Testaments Betrayed

An Essay in Nine Parts

Milan Kundera

*Translated from the French
by Linda Asher*

faber and faber

First published in the USA in 1995
by HarperCollins Publishers, Inc.
First published in Great Britain 1995
by Faber and Faber Limited
Bloomsbury House
74-77 Great Russell Street
London WC1B 3DA.
Originally published in France
under the title *Les testaments trahis*.
This UK paperback edition first published in 1996.

Printed in the UK by CPI Bookmarque, Croydon

© Milan Kundera, 1993
Translation copyright © Linda Asher, 1995

Linda Asher is hereby identified as translator of this work
in accordance with Section 77 of the Copyright,
Designs and Patents Act 1988.

A CIP record for this book
is available from the British Library

ISBN 0-571-17337-3

700.1

6 8 10 9 7 5

PART ONE

*The Day Panurge No Longer
Makes People Laugh*

The Invention of Humor

The pregnant Madame Grandgousier ate too much tripe, and they had to give her a purgative; it was so strong that the placenta let go, the fetus Gargantua slipped into a vein, traveled up her system, and came out of his mama's ear. From the very first lines, Rabelais's book shows its hand: the story being told here is not serious: that is, there are no statements of truths here (scientific or mythic); no promise to describe things as they are in reality.

Rabelais's time was fortunate: the novel as butterfly is taking flight, carrying the shreds of the chrysalis on its back. With his giant form, Pantagruel still belongs to the past of fantastic tales, while Panurge comes from the yet unknown future of the novel. The extraordinary moment of the birth of a new art gives Rabelais's book an astounding richness; it has everything: the plausible and the implausible, allegory, satire, giants and ordinary men, anecdotes, meditations, voyages real and fantastic, scholarly disputes, digressions of pure verbal virtuosity. Today's novelist, with his legacy from the nineteenth century, feels an envious nostalgia for the superbly heterogeneous universe of those earliest novelists and for the delightful liberty with which they dwelt in it.

Just as Rabelais starts his book by dropping Gargantua onto the world's stage from his mama's ear, so in *The Satanic Verses*, after a midair plane explosion, do Salman Rushdie's two heroes fall through the air chattering, singing, and carrying on in comic and improbable fashion. While "above, behind, below them in the void" float reclining seats, paper cups, oxygen masks, and passengers, one of them—Gibreel Farishta—swims "in air, butterfly-stroke, breast-stroke, bunching himself into a ball, spreadeagling himself against the almost-infinity of the almost-dawn," and the other—Saladin Chamcha—like "a fastidious shadow falling headfirst in a grey suit with all the jacket buttons done up, arms by his sides. . . a bowler hat on his head." The novel opens with that scene, for, like Rabelais, Rushdie knows that the contract between the novelist and the reader must be established from the outset; it must be clear: the story being told here is not serious, even though it is about the most dreadful things.

The marriage of the not-serious and the dreadful: witness this scene from Rabelais's *Fourth Book*: on the open sea, Pantagruel's boat meets a ship full of sheep merchants; one of them, seeing Panurge with no codpiece and with his eyeglasses fastened to his hat, takes the liberty of talking big and calls him a cuckold. Panurge is quick to retaliate: he buys a sheep from the fellow and throws it into the sea; it being their nature to follow the leader, all the other sheep start jumping into the water. In a panic, the merchants grab hold of the sheeps' fleece and horns, and are dragged into the sea themselves. Panurge picks up an oar, not to save them but to keep them from climbing back onto the ship; eloquently, he exhorts them, describing the miseries of this world and the benefits and delights of the next, declaring that the dead are more fortunate than the living. Even so, should they by some chance prefer to go on living among humans, he wishes them a meeting with some whale, like Jonah. The mass drowning accomplished, the good Frère Jean congratulates Panurge, only reproaching him for having paid the merchant beforehand and thus thrown away money. Says Panurge: "By God, I got a good fifty thousand francs' worth of fun for it!"

The scene is unreal, impossible; does it, at least, have a moral? Is Rabelais denouncing the stinginess of the merchants, whose punishment should please us? Or does he mean to make us indignant at Panurge's cruelty? Or, as a good anticlerical, is he mocking the stupidity of the religious clichés Panurge recites? Guess! Every answer is a booby trap.

Says Octavio Paz: "There is no humor in Homer or Virgil; Ariosto seems to foreshadow it, but not until Cervantes does humor take shape. . . . Humor," he goes on, "is the great invention of the modern spirit." A fundamental idea: humor is not an age-old human practice; it is an *invention* bound up with the birth of the novel. Thus humor is not laughter, not mockery, not satire, but a particular species of the comic, which, Paz says (and this is the key to understanding humor's

essence), "renders ambiguous everything it touches."
People who cannot take pleasure from the spectacle of
Panurge letting the sheep merchants drown while he
sings them the praises of the hereafter will never
understand a thing about the art of the novel.

The Realm Where Moral Judgment
Is Suspended

If I were asked the most common cause of misunderstanding between my readers and me, I would not hesitate: humor. I had only recently come to France, and I
was anything but blasé. When a famous professor of
medicine asked to meet me because he admired
Farewell Waltz, I was most flattered. According to him,
my novel was prophetic; in my character Skreta, a
doctor who treats apparently sterile women at a spa by
injecting them secretly with his own sperm from a spe-
cial syringe, I have hit on the great issue of the future.
The professor invites me to a conference on artificial
insemination. He pulls a sheet of paper from his
pocket and reads me the draft of his own presentation.
The gift of sperm must be anonymous, free of charge,
and (here he looks me in the eye) impelled by a threefold love: love for an unknown ovum that seeks to
accomplish its mission; the donor's love for his own
individuality, which is to be perpetuated by the dona-
tion; and, third, love for a couple that is suffering,
unfulfilled. Then he looks me in the eye again: much
as he admires my work, he does have one criticism: I
did not manage to express powerfully enough the
moral beauty of the gift of semen. I defend myself: this

6

is a comic novel! My Doctor Skreta is an oddball! You shouldn't be taking it all so seriously! "So," he says, suspicious, "your novels aren't meant to be taken seriously?" I am baffled, and suddenly I realize: there is nothing harder to explain than humor.

In *The Fourth Book*, there is a storm at sea. Everyone is on deck struggling to save the ship. All except Panurge, paralyzed with fear, who just whimpers: his great lamentations go on for pages. When the storm abates, his courage returns and he bawls all of them out for their laziness. And this is what's odd: not only does this coward, this liar, this faker, provoke no indignation, but it is at the peak of his braggadocio that we love him most. These are the passages wherein Rabelais's book becomes fully and radically a *novel*: that is, a *realm where moral judgment is suspended*.

Suspending moral judgment is not the immorality of the novel; it is its *morality*. The morality that stands against the ineradicable human habit of judging instantly, ceaselessly, and everyone; of judging before, and in the absence of, understanding. From the viewpoint of the novel's wisdom, that fervid readiness to judge is the most detestable stupidity, the most pernicious evil. Not that the novelist utterly denies that moral judgment is legitimate, but that he refuses it a place in the novel. If you like, you can accuse Panurge of cowardice, accuse Emma Bovary, accuse Rastignac—that's your business; the novelist has nothing to do with it.

Creating the imaginary terrain where moral judgment is suspended was a move of enormous significance: only there could novelistic characters develop— that is, individuals conceived not as a function of some preexistent truth, as examples of good or evil, or as representations of objective laws in conflict, but as autonomous beings grounded in their own morality, in their own laws. Western society habitually presents itself as the society of the rights of man; but before a man could have rights, he had to constitute himself as an individual, to consider himself such and to be considered such; that could not happen without the long experience of the European arts and particularly of the art of the novel, which teaches the reader to be curious about others and to try to comprehend truths that differ from his own. In this sense E. M. Cioran is right to call European society "the society of the novel" and to speak of Europeans as "the children of the novel."

Profanation

The removal of gods from the world is one of the phenomena that characterize the Modern Era. The removal of gods does not mean atheism, it denotes the situation in which the individual, the thinking ego, supplants God as the basis for all things; man may continue to keep his faith, to kneel in church, to pray at his bed, but his piety shall henceforward pertain only to his subjective universe. Having described this situation, Heidegger concludes: "And thus the gods eventually departed. The resulting void is filled by the historical and psychological exploration of myths."

The historical and psychological exploration of myths, of sacred texts, means: rendering them profane, profaning them. "Profane" comes from the Latin *profanum*: the place in front of the temple, outside the temple. Profanation is thus the removal of the sacred out of the temple, to a sphere outside religion. Insofar as laughter invisibly pervades the air of the novel, profanation by novel is the worst there is. For religion and humor are incompatible.

Thomas Mann's tetralogy, *Joseph and His Brothers*, written between 1926 and 1942, is an excellent "historical and psychological exploration" of sacred texts, which, recounted in Mann's smiling and sublimely tedious tone, instantly cease to be sacred: God, who in the Bible exists for all eternity, becomes in Mann's work a human creation, the invention of Abraham, who brought him out of the polytheistic chaos as a deity who is at first superior, then unique; recognizing to whom he owes his existence, God cries: "It's unbelievable how well that dust-dumpling knows Me! I'm starting to make a name through him! Truly, I'm going to anoint him!" But above all: Mann emphasizes that his novel is a humorous work. The Holy Scriptures making us laugh! As in the story of Joseph and Potiphar's wife: crazy with love, the woman bites her tongue and then pronounces her seductive lines lisping like a baby, "thleep with me, thleep with me," while the chaste Joseph, day after day for three years, explains patiently to the lisper that they are forbidden to make love. On the fateful day, they are alone in the house; she starts up again, demanding "thleep with me, thleep with me," and he yet again patiently, pedantically explains why they must not make love, but as he explains he gets hard, harder, my God he gets so superbly hard that Potiphar's wife is driven

9

mad by the sight; she rips his garment off him, and when Joseph runs away, still with his erection, she—demented, desperate, enraged—howls and shouts for help, accusing Joseph of rape.

Mann's novel won universal respect; proof that profanity was no longer considered an offense but was henceforward an element of customary behavior. Over the course of the Modern Era, nonbelief ceased to be defiant and provocative, and belief, for its part, lost its previous missionary or intolerant certainty. The shock of Stalinism played the decisive role in this evolution: in its effort to erase Christian memory altogether, it made brutally clear that all of us—believers and nonbelievers, blasphemers and worshipers—belong to the same culture, rooted in the Christian past, without which we would be mere shadows without substance, debaters without a vocabulary, spiritually stateless.

I was raised an atheist and that suited me until the day when, in the darkest years of Communism, I saw Christians being bullied. On the instant, the provocative, zestful atheism of my early youth vanished like some juvenile brainlessness. I understood my believing friends and, carried away by solidarity and by emotion, I sometimes went along with them to mass. Still, I never arrived at the conviction that a God existed as a being that directs our destinies. Anyhow, what could I know about it? And they, what could they know? Were they sure they were sure? I was sitting in church with the strange and happy sensation that my nonbelief and their belief were oddly close.

The Well of the Past

What is an individual? Wherein does his identity reside? All novels seek to answer these questions. By what, exactly, is the self defined? By what a character does, by his actions? Yet action gets away from its author, almost always turns on him. By his mental life, then? By his thoughts, by his hidden feelings? But is a man capable of self-understanding? Can his secret thoughts be a key to his identity? Or, rather, is man defined by his vision of the world, by his ideas, by his *Weltanschauung*? This is Dostoyevsky's aesthetic: his characters are rooted in a very distinctive personal ideology, according to which they act with unbending logic. For Tolstoy, on the other hand, personal ideology is far from a stable basis for personal identity: "Stepan Arkadievich chose neither his attitudes nor his opinions, no, the attitudes and opinions came to him on their own, just as he chose neither the style of his hats nor of his coats but got what people were wearing" (*Anna Karenina*). But if personal thought is not the basis of an individual's identity (if it has no more importance than a hat), then where do we find that basis?

To this unending investigation, Thomas Mann brought his very important contribution: we think we act, we think we think, but it is another or others who think and act in us: that is to say, timeless habits, archetypes, which—having become myths passed on from one generation to the next—carry an enormous seductive power and control us (says Mann) from "the well of the past."

Thomas Mann: "Is man's 'self' narrowly limited and sealed tight within his fleshly ephemeral boundaries? Don't many of his constituent elements come from the universe outside and previous to him? . . . The distinction between mind in general and individual mind did not preoccupy people in the past nearly so powerfully as it does us today. . . ." And again: "We may be seeing a phenomenon which we would be tempted to describe as imitation or continuation, a notion of life in which each person's role is to revive certain given forms, certain mythical schema established by forebears, and to allow them reincarnation."

The conflict between Jacob and his brother Esau is only a replay of the old rivalry between Abel and his brother Cain, between God's favorite and the neglected, jealous one. This conflict, this "mythical schema established by forebears," finds its new avatar in the destiny of Jacob's son Joseph, himself one of the favored. Impelled by the immemorial sense of the favored one as culpable, Jacob sends Joseph to reconcile with his jealous brothers (an ill-fated move: they will cast him into a well).

Even suffering, that seemingly ungovernable reaction, is only "imitation and continuation": when the novel gives us the words and behavior of Jacob mourning Joseph's death, Mann comments: "This was not his usual style of speech. . . . Noah had previously used analogous or similar language about the flood, and Jacob adopted it. . . . His despair was expressed in formulas that were more or less traditional . . . though this should not cast the slightest doubt on his spontaneity." An important note: imitation does not mean lack of authenticity, for the individual cannot do otherwise than imitate what has already happened; sincere as he may be, he is only a reincarnation; truthful as he may be, he is only a sum of the suggestions and requirements that emanate from the well of the past.

Coexistence of Various Historical Periods Within a Novel

I think back to the time when I was beginning to write *The Joke*: from the start, and very spontaneously, I knew that through the character Jaroslav the novel would cast its gaze into the depths of the past (the past of folk art) and that the "I" of my character would be revealed in and by this gaze. In fact, all four protagonists are created that way: four personal communist universes grafted onto four European pasts: Ludvik: the communism that springs from the caustic Voltairean spirit; Jaroslav: communism as the desire to reconstruct the patriarchal past that is preserved in folklore; Kostka: communist utopia grafted onto the Gospel; Helena: communism as the wellspring of enthusiasm in a *homo sentimentalis*. Each of these personal universes is caught at the moment of its dissolution: four forms of communism's disintegration; which also means the collapse of four ancient European ventures.

In *The Joke*, the past appears only as a facet of the characters' psyches, or in essayistic digressions; later, I wanted to put it directly on stage. In *Life Is Elsewhere*, I set the life of a young poet of our time against the backdrop of the whole history of European poetry so that his own footsteps should mingle with those of Rimbaud, of Keats, of Lermontov. And I went still further, in this mingling of different historical periods, in *Immortality*.

As a young writer, in Prague, I detested the word "generation," whose smell of the herd put me off. The first time I had the sense of being connected to others was later, in France, reading *Terra Nostra* by Carlos Fuentes. How was it possible that someone from another continent, so distant from me in itinerary and background, should be possessed by the same aesthetic obsession to bring different historical periods to coexist in a novel, an obsession that till then I had naïvely considered to be mine alone?

Impossible to grasp the nature of the *terra nostra*, the *terra nostra* of Mexico, without looking down into the well of the past. Not as a historian would do, in order to see the chronological unfolding of events, but in order to consider: what does the *concentrated essence* of the Mexican *terra* mean to a man? Fuentes grasped that essence in the form of a dream novel where various historical periods telescope into a kind of poetic and oneiric metahistory; he thus created something almost indescribable and, in any case, hitherto unknown to literature.

That same gaze into the depths of the past I also find in *The Satanic Verses*: the complicated identity of a Europeanized Indian; *terra non nostra*; *terrae non nostrae*; *terrae perditae*; to grasp that shredded identity, the novel explores it in different locations on the planet: in London, in Bombay, in a Pakistani village, and then in seventh-century Asia.

Can this aesthetic intention (to bring together several periods in one novel) be explained by some influence on one another? No. By influences undergone in common? I cannot see what they might be. Or have we all breathed the same air of history? Has the history of the novel, by its own logic, set us all the same task?

The History of the Novel as Revenge on History Itself

History. Can we still draw on that obsolete authority? What I am about to say is a purely personal avowal: as a novelist, I have always felt myself to be within history, that is to say, partway along a road, in dialogue with those who preceded me and even perhaps (but less so) with those still to come. Of course, I am speaking of the history of the novel, not of some other history, and speaking of it such as I see it: it has nothing to do with Hegel's extrahuman reason; it is neither predetermined nor identical with the idea of progress; it is entirely human, made by men, by *some* men, and thus comparable to the development of an individual artist, who acts sometimes tritely and then surprisingly, sometimes with genius and then not, and who often misses opportunities.

Here I am making a declaration of involvement in the history of the novel, when all my novels breathe a hatred of history, of that hostile, inhuman force that—uninvited, unwanted—invades our lives from the outside and destroys them. Yet there is nothing inconsistent in this double attitude, because the history of humanity and the history of the novel are two very different things. The former is not man's to determine, it takes over like an alien force he cannot control, whereas the history of the novel (or of painting, of music) is born of man's freedom, of his wholly personal creations, of his own choices. The meaning of an art's history is opposed to the meaning of history itself. Because of its personal nature, the history of an art is a revenge by man against the impersonality of the history of humanity.

The personal nature of the history of the novel? But if it is to form a whole over the course of centuries, would not such a history need to be unified by some common and enduring—and thus by definition suprapersonal—meaning? No. I believe that even this common meaning is still personal, human; for over the course of history the concept of this or that art (what is the novel?), as well as the meaning of its evolution (where has it come from and where is it going?), is constantly defined and redefined by each artist, by each new work. The meaning of the history of the novel is the very search for that meaning, its perpetual creation and re-creation, which always retroactively encompasses the whole past of the novel: Rabelais certainly never called his *Gargantua-Pantagruel* a novel. It *wasn't* a novel; it *became* one gradually as later novelists (Sterne, Diderot, Balzac, Flaubert, Vancura, Gombrowicz, Rushdie, Kis, Chamoiseau) took their inspiration from it, openly drew on it, thus integrating it into the history of the novel, or, rather, acknowledging it as the first building block in that history.

This said, the words "the end of history" have never stirred me to anguish or displeasure. "How delightful it would be to forget what it is that dries up the sap of our brief lives so as to enslave them to its useless work, how beautiful it would be to forget History!" (*Life Is Elsewhere*) If history is going to end (though I cannot imagine in concrete terms that "end" the philosophers love to talk about), then let it happen fast! But applied to art, that same phrase, "the end of history," strikes me with terror; that end I can imagine only too well, for most novels produced today stand outside the history of the novel: novelized confessions, novelized journalism, novelized score-settling, novelized autobiographies, novelized indiscretions, novelized denunciations, novelized political arguments, novelized deaths of husbands, novelized deaths of fathers, novelized deaths of mothers, novelized deflowerings, novelized childbirths—novels ad infinitum, to the end of time, that say nothing new, have no aesthetic ambition, bring no change to our understanding of man or to novelistic form, are each one like the next, are completely consumable in the morning and completely discardable in the afternoon.

To my mind, great works can only be born within the history of their art and as *participants* in that history. It is only inside history that we can see what is new and what is repetitive, what is discovery and what is imitation; in other words, only inside history can a work exist as a *value* capable of being discerned and judged. Nothing seems to me worse for art than to fall outside its own history, for it is a fall into the chaos where aesthetic values can no longer be perceived.

Improvisation and Composition

The freedom by which Rabelais, Cervantes, Diderot, Sterne enchant us had to do with improvisation. The art of complex and rigorous composition did not become a commanding need until the first half of the nineteenth century. The novel's form as it came into being then, with its action concentrated in a narrow time span, at a crossroads where many stories of many characters intersect, demanded a minutely calculated scheme of the plot lines and scenes: before beginning to write, the novelist therefore drafted and redrafted the scheme of the novel, calculated and recalculated it, designed and redesigned as that had never been done before. One need only leaf through Dostoyevsky's notes for *The Possessed*: in the seven notebooks that take up 400 pages of the Pléiade edition (the novel itself takes up 750), motifs look for characters, characters look for motifs, characters vie for the status of protagonist; Stavrogin should be married, but "to whom?" wonders Dostoyevsky, and he tries to marry him successively to three women; and so on. (A paradox that only seems one: the more calculated the construction machinery, the more real and natural the characters. The prejudice against constructional thinking as a "nonartistic" element that mutilates the "living" quality of characters is just sentimental naïveté from people who have never understood art.)

The novelist in our time who is nostalgic for the art of the old masters of the novel cannot retie the thread where it was cut; he cannot leap over the enormous experience of the nineteenth century; if he wants to connect with the easygoing freedom of Rabelais or Sterne, he must reconcile it with the requirements of composition.

I remember my first reading of *Jacques le Fataliste*; delighted by its boldly heterogeneous richness, where ideas mingle with anecdote, where one story frames another; delighted by a freedom of composition that utterly ignores the rule about unity of action, I asked myself: Is this magnificent disorder the effect of admirable construction, subtly calculated, or is it due to the euphoria of pure improvisation? Without a doubt, it is improvisation that prevails here; but the question I spontaneously asked showed me that a prodigious architectural potential exists within such intoxicated improvisation, the potential for a complex, rich structure that would also be as perfectly calculated, calibrated, and premeditated as even the most exuberant architectural fantasy of a cathedral was necessarily premeditated. Does such an architectural intention cause a novel to lose the charm of its liberty? Its quality of game? But just what is a game, actually? Every game is based on rules, and the stricter the rules, the more the game is a game. As opposed to the chess player, the artist invents his own rules for himself; so when he improvises without rules, he is no freer than when he invents his own system of rules.

Reconciling Rabelais's and Diderot's freedom with the demands of composition, though, presents the twentieth-century novelist with problems different from those that preoccupied Balzac or Dostoyevsky. For example: the third and last of the books that constitute Hermann Broch's novel *The Sleepwalkers* is a "polyphonic" stream composed of five "voices," five entirely independent lines: neither a common action nor the same characters tie these lines together, and each has a completely different formal nature (A = novel, B = reportage, C = short story, D = poetry, E = essay). In the eighty-eight chapters of the book, these five lines alternate in this strange order: A-A-A-B-A-B-

A-C-A-A-D-E-C-A-B-D-C-D-A-E-A-A-B-E-C-A-D-B-
B-A-E-A-A-E-A-B-D-C-B-B-D-A-B-E-A-A-B-A-D-A-
C-B-D-A-E-B-A-D-A-B-D-E-A-C-A-D-D-B-A-A-C-D-
E-B-A-B-D-B-A-B-A-A-D-A-A-D-D-E.

What is it that led Broch to choose precisely this
order rather than another? What made him take precisely line B in the fourth chapter and not C or D? Not
the logic of the characters or of the action, for there is
no action common to these five lines. He was guided
by other criteria: by the charm that comes from surprising juxtaposition of the different forms (verse, narration, aphorisms, philosophical meditations); by the
contrast of different emotions pervading the different
chapters; by the variety of the chapters' lengths;
finally, by the development of the same existential
questions, reflected in the five lines as in five mirrors.
For lack of a better term, let us call these criteria *musical* and conclude: the nineteenth century elaborated
the art of composition, but our own century brought
musicality to that art.

The Satanic Verses is constructed of three more or
less independent lines: A: the lives of Saladin Chamcha
and Gibreel Farishta, two present-day Indians who
divide their time between Bombay and London; B: the
Koranic story dealing with the origin of Islam; C: the
villagers' trek toward Mecca across the sea they believe
they will cross dry-footed and in which they drown.

The three lines are taken up in sequence in the
novel's nine parts in the following order: A-B-A-C-A-
B-A-C-A (incidentally: in music, a sequence of this
kind is called a rondo: the main theme returns regularly, in alternation with several secondary themes).

This is the rhythm of the whole (I note parenthetically the approximate number of pages): A (90), B (40), A (80), C (40), A (120), B (40), A (80), C (40), A (40). It can be seen that the B and C parts are all the same length, which gives the whole a rhythmic regularity.

Line A takes up five sevenths of the novel's page total, and lines B and C one seventh each. This quantitative ratio results in the dominance of line A: the novel's center of gravity is located in the present-day lives of Farishta and Chamcha.

Nonetheless, even though B and C are subordinate lines, it is in them that the *aesthetic wager* of the novel is concentrated, for it is these B and C parts that enable Rushdie to get at the fundamental problem of all novels (that of an individual's, a character's, identity) in a new way that goes beyond the conventions of the psychological novel: Chamcha's and Farishta's personalities cannot be apprehended through a detailed description of their states of mind; their mystery lies in the cohabitation in their psyches of two civilizations, the Indian and the European; it lies in their roots, from which they have been torn but which, nevertheless, remain alive in them. Where is the rupture in these roots and how far down must one go to touch the wound? Looking into "the well of the past" is not off the point; it aims directly at the heart of the matter: the existential rift in the two protagonists.

Just as Jacob is incomprehensible without Abraham (who, according to Mann, lived centuries before him), being merely his "imitation and continuation," Gibreel Farishta is incomprehensible without the Archangel Gibreel, without Mahound (Mohammed), incomprehensible even without the theocratic Islam of Khomeini or of that fanatical girl who leads the villagers to Mecca, or rather to death. They are all his own potentialities, which sleep within him and which he must battle for his own individuality. In this novel, there is no important question that can be examined without looking down the well of the past. What is good and what is evil? Who is the other's devil, Chamcha for Farishta or Farishta for Chamcha? Is it the devil or the angel that has inspired the pilgrimage of the villagers? Is their drowning a piteous disaster or the glorious journey to Paradise? Who can say? Who can know? And what if this unknowability of good and evil was the torment suffered by the founders of religions? Those terrible words of despair, Christ's unprecedented blasphemy, "My God, my God, why hast thou forsaken me?": do they not resound in the soul of every Christian? Mahound's doubt as he wonders who put those verses into his head, God or the devil: does it not conceal the uncertainty that is the ground of man's very existence?

In the Shadow of Great Principles

Starting with his *Midnight's Children*, which in its time (in 1980) stirred unanimous admiration, no one in the English-language literary world has denied that Rushdie is one of the most gifted novelists of our day. *The Satanic Verses*, appearing in English in September 1988, was greeted with the attention due a major writer. The book received these tributes with no anticipation of the storm that was to burst some months later, when the Imam Khomeini, the master of Iran, condemned Rushdie to death for blasphemy and sent killers after him on a chase whose end no one can predict.

That happened before the text could be translated. Thus everywhere except in the English-language world, the scandal arrived before the book. In France, the press immediately printed excerpts from the still unpublished novel to show the reasons for the condemnation. Completely normal behavior, but fatal for a novel. Represented exclusively by its *incriminated* passages, it was, from the beginning, transformed from a work of art into a simple *corpus delicti*.

We should not denigrate literary criticism. Nothing is worse for a writer than to come up against its absence. I am speaking of literary criticism as meditation, as analysis; literary criticism that involves several readings of the book it means to discuss (like great pieces of music we can listen to time and again, great novels too are made for repeated readings); literary criticism that, deaf to the implacable clock of topicality, will readily discuss works a year, thirty years, three hundred years old; literary criticism that tries to apprehend the originality of a work in order thus to inscribe it on historical memory. If such meditation did not accompany the history of the novel, we would know nothing today of Dostoyevsky, or Joyce, or Proust. For without it a work is surrendered to completely arbitrary judgments and swift oblivion. Now, the Rushdie case shows (if proof is still needed) that such meditation is no longer practiced. Imperceptibly, innocently, under the pressure of events, through changes in society and in the press, literary criticism has become a mere (often intelligent, always hasty) *literary news bulletin.*

About *The Satanic Verses*, the literary news was the death sentence on the author. In such a life-and-death situation, it seems almost frivolous to speak of art. What is art, after all, when great principles are under attack? Thus, throughout the world, all discussion concentrated on questions of principle: freedom of expression; the need to defend it (and indeed people did defend it, people protested, people signed petitions); religion; Islam and Christianity; but also this question: does a writer have the moral right to blaspheme and thereby wound believers? And even this problem: suppose Rushdie had attacked Islam only for publicity and to sell his unreadable book?

With mysterious unanimity (I noticed the same reaction everywhere in the world), the men of letters, the intellectuals, the salon initiates, snubbed the novel. They decided to resist all commercial pressure for once, and they refused to read a work they considered simply a piece of sensationalism. They signed all the petitions for Rushdie, meanwhile deeming it elegant to say, with a supercilious smile: "His book? Oh no, no, no! I haven't read it." The politicians took advantage of this curious "state of disgrace" of a novelist they didn't like. I'll never forget the virtuous impartiality they paraded at the time: "We condemn Khomeini's verdict. Freedom of expression is sacred to us. But no less do we condemn this attack on religious faith. It is a shameful, contemptible attack that insults the soul of peoples."

Of course, no one any longer doubted that Rushdie actually had *attacked* Islam, for only the accusation was real; the text of the book no longer mattered, it no longer existed.

The Clash of Three Eras

A situation unique in history: Rushdie belongs by origin to a Muslim society that, in large part, is still living in the period before the Modern Era. He wrote his book in Europe, in the Modern Era—or, more precisely, at the end of that era.

Just as Iranian Islam was at the time moving away from religious moderation toward a combative theocracy, so, with Rushdie, the history of the novel was moving from the genteel, professorial smile of Thomas Mann to unbridled imagination drawn from the rediscovered wellspring of Rabelaisian humor. The antitheses collided, each in its extreme form.

From this viewpoint, the condemnation of Rushdie can be seen not as a chance event, an aberration, but as the most profound conflict between two eras: theocracy goes to war against the Modern Era and targets its most representative creation: the novel. For Rushdie did not blaspheme. He did not attack Islam. He wrote a novel. But that, for the theocratic mind, is worse than an attack: if a religion is attacked (by a polemic, a blasphemy, a heresy), the guardians of the temple can easily defend it on their own ground, with their own language; but the novel is a different planet for them; a different universe based on a different ontology; an *infernum* where the unique truth is powerless and where satanic ambiguity turns every certainty into enigma.

Let us emphasize this: not attack but ambiguity.

The second part of *The Satanic Verses* (the incriminated part, which evokes Mohammed and the origin of Islam) is presented in the novel as a *dream* of Gibreel Farishta's, who then develops the dream into a cheap movie in which he himself will play the role of the archangel. The story is thus *doubly* relativized (first as a dream, then as a *bad* film that will flop) and presented not as a declaration but as a *playful invention*. A disagreeable invention? I say no: it showed me, for the first time in my life, the *poetry* of the Islamic religion, of the Islamic world.

We should stress this: there is no place for hatred in the relativistic universe of the novel: the author who writes a novel in order to settle scores (personal or ideological) is headed for total and certain aesthetic ruin. Ayesha, the girl who leads the hallucinating villagers to their deaths, is of course a monster, but she is also seductive, wondrous (haloed by the butterflies that accompany her everywhere), and often touching; even in the portrait of an émigré imam (an imaginary portrait of Khomeini), there is an almost respectful understanding; Western modernity is viewed with skepticism, never presented as superior to Oriental archaism; the novel "historically and psychologically explores" sacred old texts, but it also shows how much they are *degraded* by TV, advertising, the entertainment industry; and the left-wing characters, who deplore the frivolity of this modern world—do they at least enjoy the author's full sympathy? No indeed, they are miserably ridiculous, and as frivolous as the frivolity around them; no one is right and no one entirely wrong in the immense *carnival of relativity* that is this work.

Therefore, with *The Satanic Verses*, the art of the

novel as such is incriminated. That is why, in this whole sad story, the saddest thing is not Khomeini's verdict (which proceeds from a logic that is atrocious but consistent); rather, it is Europe's incapacity to defend and explain (explain patiently to itself and to others) that most European of the arts, the art of the novel; in other words, to explain and defend its own culture. The "children of the novel" have abandoned the art that shaped them. Europe, the "society of the novel," has abandoned its own self.

It does not surprise me that the Sorbonne theologians, the sixteenth-century ideological police who kindled so many stakes, should have made life so hard for Rabelais, forcing him often to flee and hide. What seems to me far more amazing and admirable is the protection provided him by the powerful men of his time, Cardinal du Bellay, for instance, and Cardinal Odet, and above all François I, the king of France. Were they seeking to defend principles? Freedom of expression? Human rights? They had a better motive: they loved literature and the arts.

I see no Cardinal du Bellay, no François I, in today's Europe. But is Europe still Europe? Is it still "the society of the novel"? In other words, is it still living in the Modern Era? Or is it already moving into another era, as yet unnamed, for which its arts are no longer of much importance? If that is so, why be surprised that Europe was not disturbed beyond measure when, for the first time in its history, the art of the novel—*Europe's* art par excellence—was condemned to death? In this new age, after the Modern Era, has not the novel for some time already been living on death row?

The European Novel

To define precisely the art I am discussing, I call it the *European novel*. By that I mean not only novels created in Europe by Europeans but novels that belong to a history that began with the dawn of the Modern Era in Europe. There are of course other novels, the novel of China, of Japan, the novel of ancient Greece, but they are not bound by any continuous evolutionary line to the historical enterprise that began with Rabelais and Cervantes.

I speak of the *European novel* not only to distinguish it from, say, the Chinese novel but also to point out that its history is transnational; that the French novel, the English novel, the Hungarian novel, are in no position to create autonomous histories of their own but are all part of a common, supranational history that provides the only context capable of revealing both the direction of the novel's evolution and the value of particular works.

At different phases of that evolution, different nations, as in a relay race, took the initiative: first Italy with Boccaccio, the great precursor; then France with Rabelais, and Spain with Cervantes and the picaresque novel; the English novel in the eighteenth century and then, toward the century's end, the German contribution, with Goethe; the nineteenth century, which belonged almost entirely to France, along with the Russian novel in the last third, and, immediately thereafter, the arrival of the Scandinavian novel. Then the twentieth century and its Central European adventure with Kafka, Musil, Broch, and Gombrowicz. . .

If Europe were only a single nation, I do not believe

the history of its novel could have lasted with such vitality, such power, and such diversity for four centuries. It was the ever new historical situations (with their new existential content), arising in France, then in Russia, then elsewhere, and somewhere else again, that kept the art of the novel going, brought it new inspirations, suggested new aesthetic solutions. It is as if in the course of its journey the history of the novel kept waking the different parts of Europe, one after the other, confirming them in their specificity and at the same time integrating them into a common European consciousness.

In our own century, for the first time, the important initiatives in the history of the European novel are appearing outside Europe: first in North America, in the 1920s and '30s, and then, in the '60s, in Latin America. What with the pleasure provided me by the art of the French-speaking Antillean novelist Patrick Chamoiseau, and then by Rushdie's, I would prefer to speak more generally of the *novel from below the thirty-fifth parallel*, the *novel of the South*: a great new novelistic culture characterized by an extraordinary sense of the real coupled with an untrammeled imagination that breaks every rule of plausibility.

I am delighted by that imagination without understanding completely where it comes from. Kafka? Certainly. For our century, it is he who gave legitimacy to the implausible in the art of the novel. Yet the Kafkan imagination is different from Rushdie's or García Márquez's; that teeming imagination seems rooted in the very specific culture of the South; for example, in its still living oral literature (Chamoiseau drawing inspiration from the Creole storytellers) or, as

Fuentes likes to recall, in the Latin American Baroque, more exuberant, more "crazy," than Europe's.

Or another key to that imagination: the *tropicalization of the novel*. I refer to Rushdie's fantasy: Farishta hovers above London and wishes to "tropicalize" that hostile city. He lists the advantages of tropicalization: "institution of a national siesta . . . new birds in the trees (macaws, peacocks, cockatoos), new trees under the birds (coco-palms, tamarind, banyans with hanging beards) . . . religious fervour, political ferment . . . friends to commence dropping in on one another without making appointments, closure of old folks' homes, emphasis on the extended family . . . spicier food. . . . Disadvantages: cholera, typhoid, legionnaires' disease, cockroaches, dust, noise, a culture of excess."

("Culture of excess" is an excellent expression. The tendency of the novel in the last stages of its modernism: in Europe: the ordinary pursued to its utmost; sophisticated analysis of gray on gray; outside Europe: accumulation of the most extraordinary coincidences; colors on colors. The dangers: in Europe, tedium of gray; outside Europe, monotony of the picturesque.)

The novels created below the thirty-fifth parallel, though a bit foreign to European taste, are the extension of the history of the European novel, of its form and of its spirit, and are even astonishingly close to its earliest beginnings; nowhere else today does the old Rabelaisian sap run so joyfully as in the work of these non-European writers.

The Day Panurge No Longer Makes People Laugh

Which brings me back one last time to Panurge. In *Pantagruel*, he falls in love with a woman and is determined to have her at all costs. In church, during mass (isn't that a hell of a sacrilege!), he addresses her with some outrageous obscenities (in today's America, such "verbal rape" would cost him dear) and, when she refuses to listen, takes his revenge by sprinkling her gown with the minced genitals of a bitch in heat. As she leaves the church, all the dogs roundabout (six hundred thousand and fourteen, says Rabelais) run up and piss on her. I remember living in a workers' dormitory when I was twenty, my Rabelais in Czech translation under my bed. The men were curious about this fat book, and time and again I had to read them the story, which they soon knew by heart. Even though these were people of a rather conservative peasant mentality, their laughter hadn't a trace of condemnation for that rhetorical and urinary harasser; they adored Panurge, so much so that they gave his name to one of our companions; no, not a womanizer, but a youngster known for his naïveté and his exaggerated chastity, who was ashamed to be seen naked in the shower. I can hear their cries as if it were yesterday: "Panurk"—our Czech pronunciation of the name— "get into the shower! Or we'll wash you down with dog piss!"

I can still hear that hearty laughter, making fun of a pal's modesty but at the same time showing an almost marveling affection for it. They were delighted by the obscenities Panurge addresses to the woman in church, but equally delighted by the punishment the woman's chastity inflicted on him and then, to their great pleasure, her own punishment by the dogs' urine. With what or whom did my erstwhile companions sympathize? With modesty? With immodesty? With Panurge? With the woman? Or with the dogs who had the enviable privilege of urinating on a beauty?

Humor: the divine flash that reveals the world in its moral ambiguity and man in his profound incompetence to judge others; humor: the intoxicating relativity of human things; the strange pleasure that comes of the certainty that there is no certainty.

But humor, to recall Octavio Paz, is "the great invention of the modern spirit." It has not been with us forever, and it won't be with us forever either.

With a heavy heart, I imagine the day when Panurge no longer makes people laugh.

PART TWO

The Castrating Shadow of Saint Garta

1

The image of Kafka that is widely held these days comes originally from a novel. Max Brod wrote it immediately after Kafka's death and published it in 1926. Savor the title: *The Enchanted Kingdom of Love* (*Zauberreich der Liebe*). This key-novel is a roman à clef, a novel with a key. Its protagonist, a German writer in Prague named Nowy, is recognizably a flattering self-portrait of Brod (adored by women, envied by the literati). Nowy/Brod cuckolds a man who, by very elaborate wicked schemes, gets him sent to prison for four years. We are instantly plunged into a story cobbled together by the most improbable coincidences (characters meet by complete chance on a ship out at sea, on a Haifa street, on a street in Vienna), we witness the struggle between the good (Nowy and his mistress) and the evil (the cuckold, so vulgar that he fully deserves his horns, and a literary critic who systematically pans Nowy's wonderful books), we are pained by melodramatic reversals (the heroine kills herself because she cannot bear life caught between the cuckold and the cuckolder), we admire the sensitive soul of Nowy/Brod, who swoons regularly.

This novel would have been forgotten before it was written if not for the character Garta. Because Garta, Nowy's close friend, is a portrait of Kafka. Without this key, the character would be the most uninteresting in the entire history of literature; he is described as a "saint of our time," but even about the ministry of his saintliness we don't learn much, except that from time to time, when Nowy/Brod is having love troubles, he seeks advice from his friend, which the friend, as a saint with no such experience, is incapable of giving him.

What a marvelous paradox: the whole image of Kafka and the whole posthumous fate of his work were first conceived and laid out in this simpleminded novel, this garbage, this cartoon-novel concoction, which, aesthetically, stands at exactly the opposite pole from Kafka's art.

2

Some quotations from the novel: Garta "was a saint of our time, a veritable saint." "Perhaps his best quality was his remaining so independent and free, so saintly rational in the face of all mythologies, even though deep down he was akin to them and nearly a mythological figure himself." "He wanted to live in perfect purity—rather, he could not do otherwise. . . ."

The words "saint," "saintly," "mythological," "purity," are not a matter of rhetoric; they are to be taken literally: "Of all the sages and prophets who have walked the earth, he was the quietest. . . . Perhaps he lacked one thing: self-confidence. With it, he would have become a guide to humanity. No, he was not a guide. He spoke neither to the people nor to disciples, like the Buddha, Jesus, Moses. He did not speak that way. He remained reticent. Was that because he saw more deeply into the great mystery than those three? Because what he undertook was more difficult yet than what the Buddha intended? Because if he succeeded, it would be conclusive?"

And again: "All the founders of religions were sure of themselves. One of them, however—he may well be the most sincere of all—Lao-tze, retreated into the shadows. Garta certainly did the same."

Garta is presented as someone who writes. Nowy "had agreed to be Garta's literary executor—Garta had asked him to do this, but with the unusual condition that everything be destroyed." Nowy "sensed the reason for that last wish. Garta was not announcing a new religion; he wanted only *to live his faith*. . . . He required the ultimate effort of himself; as he had not succeeded, his writings (mere rungs to help him climb to the heights) had no value for him."

Still, Nowy/Brod did not want to obey his friend's wish, because in his view, Garta's writings, "even as attempts, as mere sketches, bring to wandering humanity a presentiment of something irreplaceable."

Yes, it's all there.

3

Were it not for Brod, we would not even know Kafka's name today. Right after his friend's death, Brod saw to the publication of his three novels. No reaction. So he realized that, to establish Kafka's work, he would have to undertake a real and long war. Establishing a body of work means presenting it, interpreting it. Brod opened a veritable artillery attack: prefaces: for *The Trial* (1925), for *The Castle* (1926), for *Amerika* (1927), for "Description of a Struggle" (1936), for the diaries and letters (1937), for the stories (1946); for the *Conversations* by Gustav Janouch (1952); then the dramatizations: of *The Castle* (1953) and *Amerika* (1957); but above all, four important books of interpretation (take good note of the titles!): *Franz Kafka: A Biography* (1937), *The Faith and Teachings of Franz Kafka* (1946), *Franz Kafka, He Who Shows the Way* (1951), and *Despair and Salvation in the Work of Franz Kafka* (1959).

Through all of these texts, the image outlined in *The Enchanted Kingdom of Love* is confirmed and developed: above all, Kafka is primarily the religious thinker, *der religiöse Denker*. True, he "never systematically set out his philosophy and his religious world view. Nonetheless, we can deduce rather clear fundamentals from his work, from his aphorisms especially but also from his poetry, his letters, his diaries, and then also from his way of life (from that above all). . . ."

Further on: Kafka's true importance cannot be understood "unless two currents in his work are distinguished: (1) the aphorisms, (2) the narrative writings (novels, stories, fragments).

"In his aphorisms Kafka expounds the positive word [*das positive Wort*] that he gives to mankind, a faith, a stern call for each individual to change his own life."

In his novels and stories, "he describes the horrible punishments in store for those who do not wish to hear the word [*das Wort*] and do not follow the path of righteousness."

Note the hierarchy: at the top: Kafka's life as an example to be followed; in the middle: the aphorisms, that is, all the meditative "philosophical" passages in his diaries; at the bottom: the narrative works.

Brod was a brilliant intellectual with exceptional energy; a generous man willing to do battle for others; his attachment to Kafka was warm and disinterested. The only problem was his artistic orientation: a man of ideas, he knew nothing of the passion for form; his novels (he wrote twenty of them) are sadly conventional; and above all: he understood nothing at all about modern art.

Why, despite all this, was Kafka so fond of him? What about you—do you stop being fond of your best friend because he has a compulsion to write bad verse?

But the man who writes bad verse turns dangerous once he starts to publish the work of his poet friend. Suppose the most influential commentator on Picasso were a painter who could not even manage to understand the impressionists. What would he say about Picasso's paintings? Probably the same thing Brod said about Kafka's novels: that they describe "the horrible punishments in store for those who . . . do not follow the path of righteousness."

4

Max Brod created the image of Kafka and that of his work; he created *Kafkology* at the same time. The Kafkologists may distance themselves from their founding father, but they never leave the terrain he mapped out for them. Despite the astronomical number of its texts, Kafkology goes on elaborating infinite variants on the same discussion, the same speculation, which, increasingly unconnected to Kafka's work, feeds only on itself. Through innumerable prefaces, postfaces, notes, biographies and monographs, university lectures and dissertations, Kafkology produces and sustains its own image of Kafka, to the point where the author whom readers know by the name Kafka is no longer Kafka but the Kafkologized Kafka.

Not everything written on Kafka is Kafkology. How then to define Kafkology? By a tautology: Kafkology is discourse for Kafkologizing Kafka. For replacing Kafka with the Kafkologized Kafka:

1) Following Brod's example, Kafkology examines Kafka's books not in the *large context* of literary history (the history of the European novel) but almost exclusively in the *microcontext* of biography. In their monograph, Boisdeffre and Albérès cite Proust rejecting biographical explication of art, but only to say that Kafka requires exception to that rule, as his books are "not separable from his person. Whether he is called Josef K., Rohan, Samsa, the Surveyor, Bendemann, Josefine the Singer, the Hunger Artist, or the Trapeze Artist, the hero of his books is none other than Kafka himself." Biography is the principal key for under-

standing the meaning of the work. Worse: the only meaning of the work is as a key for understanding the biography.

2) Following Brod's example, in the hands of the Kafkologists *Kafka's biography becomes hagiography*; such as the unforgettable bombast with which Roman Karst ended his talk at the famous 1963 conference on Kafka in Czechoslovakia: "Franz Kafka lived and suffered for us!" Various kinds of hagiography: religious; secular—Kafka, martyr to his solitude; leftist—Kafka "assiduously" attending anarchist meetings and "very interested in the 1917 Revolution" (according to a mythomaniacal assertion frequently cited but never verified). To every church its apocrypha: *Conversations with Kafka* by Gustav Janouch. To every saint a sacrificial gesture: Kafka's wish to have his work destroyed.

3) Following Brod's example, *Kafkology systematically dislodges Kafka from the domain of aesthetics*: either as a "religious thinker" or else, on the left, as a protester against art, whose "ideal library would include only books by engineers or mechanics, and declaratory jurists" (in the book by Deleuze and Guattari). Kafkology is tireless in examining his connections to Kierkegaard, to Nietzsche, to the theologians, but ignores the novelists and poets. Even Camus, in his essay, discusses Kafka in terms one would use not for a novelist but for a philosopher. His private writings are treated the same way as his novels, but with a marked preference for the former: taking at random the Kafka essay Roger Garaudy wrote while he was still a Marxist: fifty-four times he quotes Kafka's letters, Kafka's diaries forty-five times; the Janouch *Conversations* thirty-five times; the stories

twenty times; *The Trial* five times, *The Castle* four times, *Amerika* not once.

4) Following Brod's example, *Kafkology ignores the existence of modern art*; as though Kafka did not belong to the generation of the great innovators—Stravinsky, Webern, Bartók, Apollinaire, Musil, Joyce, Picasso, Braque—all born, like him, between 1880 and 1883. When, in the 1950s, someone proposed the notion of his kinship with Beckett, Brod immediately protested: Saint Garta has nothing to do with such decadence!

5) Kafkology is not literary criticism (it does not examine the value of the work: the previously unknown aspects of existence that the work reveals, the aesthetic innovations by which it affected the evolution of the art, etc.); *Kafkology is an exegesis*. As such, it can see only allegories in Kafka's novels. They are religious (Brod: the Castle = the grace of God; the surveyor = the new Parsifal in quest of the divine; etc., etc.); they are psychoanalytical, existentialistical, Marxist (the surveyor = a symbol of revolution, because he undertakes land redistribution); they are political (Orson Welles's *The Trial*). Kafkology does not look to Kafka's novels for the real world transformed by an immense imagination; rather, it decodes religious messages, it deciphers philosophical parables.

5

"Garta was a saint of our time, a veritable saint." But can a saint go to brothels? When Brod published Kafka's diaries he censored them somewhat; he deleted not only the allusions to whores but anything else touching on sex. Kafkology has always expressed doubts about its subject's virility, and it delights in discussing the martyrdom of his impotence. Thus Kafka long ago became the patron saint of the neurotic, the depressive, the anorexic, the feeble; the patron saint of the twisted, the *précieuses ridicules*, and the hysterical (in the Orson Welles film, K. howls hysterically, whereas Kafka's novels are the least hysterical in the entire history of literature).

Biographers know nothing about the sex lives of their own wives, but they think they know all about Stendhal's or Faulkner's. About Kafka's I would dare say nothing but this: the (not very easy) erotic life of his time had little resemblance to ours: girls in those days did not make love before marriage; for a bachelor, that left only two possibilities: married women of good family, or easy women of the lower classes: shop-girls, maids, and of course prostitutes.

The imagination of Brod's novels drew on the first source; whence their kind of eroticism—rapturous, romantic (involving dramatic cuckoldries, suicides, pathological jealousies), and asexual: "Women are wrong to believe a good man cares only about physical possession. That is merely a symbol and is by far less important than this feeling: the woman loves me, and so she is entirely well-disposed toward me. All of man's love seeks to win woman's good will and kindness" (*The Enchanted Kingdom of Love*).

The erotic imagination in Kafka's novels, on the contrary, draws almost exclusively on the other source: "I walked past the brothel as though it were the house of a beloved" (diary, 1910, sentence censored by Brod).

Masterful as they were at analyzing all the strategies of seduction, nineteenth-century novels left sex
and the sexual act itself hidden. In the first decades of
our century, sex emerged from the mists of romantic
passion. Kafka was one of the first (certainly along
with Joyce) to uncover it in his novels. He unveiled sex
not as the playing field for a small circle of libertines
(in eighteenth-century style) but as a commonplace,
fundamental reality in everyone's life. Kafka unveiled
the *existential* aspects of sex: sex in conflict with love;
the strangeness of the other as a condition, a requirement, of sex; the ambiguous nature of sex: those
aspects that are exciting and simultaneously repugnant; its terrible triviality, which in no way lessens its
frightening power, etc.

Brod was a romantic. By contrast, at the root of
Kafka's novels I believe I discern a profound antiro-
manticism; it shows up everywhere: in the way Kafka
sees society as well as in the way he constructs a sentence; but its origin may lie in Kafka's vision of sex.

6

Young Karl Rossmann (the protagonist of *Amerika*) is
put out of the parental home and sent to America
because of his unfortunate sexual mishap with a
housemaid, who "had seduced him and got herself a
child by him." Before the coition: "'Karl, oh my
Karl!' she exclaimed . . . while he could see nothing
at all and felt uncomfortable amid all the warm bedding that she had apparently piled on especially for
his sake. . . ." Then she "shook him, listened to his

heartbeat, offered him her chest so that he could listen to hers the same way." Next she "groped between his legs in so disgusting a manner that Karl's head and neck came thrashing out from among the pillows." But then she "pushed her belly against him several times—he felt she was a part of himself and that may be why he was overcome by a terrible need."

This minor copulation is the cause of everything to follow in the novel. Realizing that our destiny is determined by something utterly trivial is depressing. But any revelation of some unexpected triviality is a source of comedy as well. *Post coitum omne animal triste.* Kafka was the first to describe the comic side of that sadness.

The comic side of sex: an idea unacceptable to puritans and neolibertines both. I think of D. H. Lawrence, that bard of Eros, that evangelist of coition, who, in *Lady Chatterley's Lover*, tried to rehabilitate sex by making it lyrical. But lyrical sex is even more ridiculous than the lyrical sentimentality of the last century.

The erotic gem of *Amerika* is Brunelda. She fascinated Federico Fellini. For a long time, he dreamed of making a film of *Amerika*, and in his *Intervista* there is a scene that shows the casting for this dream project: a bunch of incredible candidates turn out for the role of Brunelda, women Fellini had picked with the exuberant delight he was known for. (But I say it again: that exuberant delight is the same as Kafka's. For Kafka did not *suffer* for us! He *enjoyed* himself for us!)

Brunelda, the former singer, "the very frail woman"

with "the gout in her legs." Brunelda with her plump little hands and the double chin, "immeasurably fat." Brunelda, sitting legs apart, "with the greatest effort, after many tries and frequent pauses to rest," bending over "to tug at her stocking-tops." Brunelda hitching up her dress and using the hem to dry the weeping Robinson's eyes. Brunelda unable to climb two or three steps and needing to be carried—a sight that so impresses Robinson that for the rest of his life he will sigh: "Oh God, oh God, how beautiful she was! What a woman!" Brunelda standing naked in the bathtub, moaning and complaining as Delamarche washes her down. Brunelda lying in that same tub, furiously pounding the water with her fists. Brunelda whom it takes two men two hours to get down the stairs and put in a cart, which Karl then pushes across the city to some mysterious place, probably a brothel. Brunelda in this handcart, with a shawl covering her up so well that a cop takes her for a cargo of potato sacks.

What is new about this portrait of massive ugliness is that it is alluring; morbidly alluring, ridiculously alluring, but still alluring; Brunelda is a monster of sex on the borderline between the repugnant and the exciting, and men's admiring cries are not only comic (they *are* comic, to be sure, sex *is* comic!) but at the same time entirely true. It is not surprising that Brod, that romantic worshiper of women, for whom coition was not reality but a "symbol of feeling," could see no truth to Brunelda, not the faintest shadow of real experience but only the description of "the horrible punishments in store for those who . . . do not follow the path of righteousness."

7

The finest erotic scene Kafka ever wrote is in the third chapter of *The Castle*: the act of love betwen K. and Frieda. Scarcely an hour after seeing that "unprepossessing little blonde" for the first time, he is embracing her behind the bar, "among the beer puddles and the other filth covering the floor." Filth: it is inseparable from sex, from its essence.

But immediately thereafter, in the same paragraph, Kafka sounds the poetry of sex: "There hours went by, hours of mutual breaths, of mutual heartbeats, hours in which K. continually had the feeling that he was going astray, or that he was farther inside the strange world than any person before him, in a strange world where the very air had in it no element of his native air, where one must suffocate from strangeness and where, in the midst of absurd enticements, one could do nothing but keep going, keep going astray."

The length of the coition turns into a metaphor for a walk beneath the sky of strangeness. And yet that walk is not ugliness; on the contrary, it attracts us, invites us to go on still farther, intoxicates us: it is beauty.

A few lines later: "he was far too happy to be holding Frieda in his hands, too anxiously happy as well, because it seemed to him that if Frieda were to leave him, everything he had would leave him." So is this love? No indeed, not love; if a person is banished and dispossessed of everything, then a tiny little woman he hardly knows, embraced in puddles of beer, becomes a whole universe—love has nothing to do with it.

8

In his *Manifesto of Surrealism*, André Breton speaks severely about the art of the novel. He complains that the novel is incurably hobbled by mediocrity, by banality, by everything that is contrary to poetry. He mocks its descriptions and its tiresome psychology. This criticism of the novel is immediately followed by praise of dreams. Then he ends by saying: "I believe in the eventual fusion of these two states, dream and reality, which are seemingly so contradictory, into a kind of absolute reality, a surreality, if one may so speak."

Paradox: the "fusion of dream and reality" that the surrealists proclaimed, without actually knowing how to bring it about in a great literary work, had already occurred, and in the very genre they disparaged: in Kafka's novels, written in the course of the previous decade.

It is very difficult to describe, to define, to give a name to the kind of imagination with which Kafka bewitches us. The "fusion of dream and reality"—that phrase Kafka of course never heard—is illuminating. As in another phrase dear to surrealists, Lautréamont's about the beauty in the chance encounter between an umbrella and a sewing machine: the more alien things are from one another, the more magical the light that springs from their contact. I'd like to call it a poetics of surprise; or beauty as perpetual astonishment. Or to use the notion of *density* as a criterion of value: density of imagination, density of unexpected encounters. The scene I cited, of the coition of K. and Frieda, is an example of that dizzying density: the short passage, scarcely a page long, encompasses three completely distinct existential discoveries (the existential triangle of sex) that are stunning in their swift succession: filth; the intoxicating dark beauty of strangeness; and touching, anxious yearning.

The whole third chapter is a whirlpool of the unexpected: within a fairly tight span come, one after the other: the first encounter between K. and Frieda at the inn; the extraordinarily realistic dialogue in the seduction, which is disguised because of the presence of a third person (Olga); the motif of a hole in the door (a trite motif, but it shifts away from empirical plausibility), through which K. sees Klamm sleeping behind the desk; the crowd of servants dancing with Olga; the surprising cruelty of Frieda, who runs them off with a whip, and their surprising fear as they obey her; the innkeeper, who arrives as K. hides by lying flat under the bar; the arrival of Frieda, who discovers K. on the floor and denies his presence to the innkeeper (meanwhile amorously caressing K.'s chest with her foot); the act of love interrupted by the call from Klamm, who has awakened, outside the door; Frieda's astonishingly courageous gesture of shouting to Klamm, "I'm with the surveyor!"; and then, to top it all off (and here empirical plausibility is completely abandoned): above them, on the bar counter, sit the two assistants; they were watching the couple the whole time.

9

The two assistants from the castle are probably Kafka's greatest poetic find, the marvel of his fantasy; their existence is not only infinitely astonishing, it is also packed with meanings: they are a couple of pathetic blackmailers and nuisances; but they also stand for the whole threatening "modernity" of the castle's universe: they are cops, reporters, paparazzi: agents of the total destruction of private life; they are the innocent clowns who wander across the stage as the drama proceeds; but they are also lecherous voyeurs whose presence imbues the whole novel with the sexual scent of a smutty, Kafkaesquely comic promiscuity.

But above all: the invention of these two assistants is like a lever that hoists the story into that realm where everything is at once strangely real and unreal, possible and impossible. Chapter Twelve: K., Frieda, and the two assistants camp in a grade-school class-room that they have turned into a bedroom. The teacher and the pupils come in just as the incredible ménage à quatre are starting their morning toilet: they get dressed behind the blankets hung from the parallel bars, while the children watch—amused, intrigued, curious (voyeurs themselves). It is more than the encounter of an umbrella with a sewing machine. It is the superbly incongruous encounter of two spaces: a grade-school classroom with a dubious bedroom.

This scene with its enormous comic poetry (which should head the list in an anthology of modernism in the novel) would have been unthinkable in the pre-Kafka era. Totally unthinkable. I stress this in order to make clear the full radical nature of Kafka's aesthetic revolution. I recall a conversation, by now twenty years back, with Gabriel García Márquez, who told me: "It was Kafka who showed me that it's possible to write *another way*." "Another way" means: breaking through the plausibility barrier. Not in order to escape the real world (the way the Romantics did) but to apprehend it better.

Because apprehending the real world is part of the definition of the novel: but how to both apprehend it and at the same time engage in an enchanting game of fantasy? How be rigorous in analyzing the world and at the same time be irresponsibly free at playful reveries? How bring these two incompatible purposes together? Kafka managed to solve this enormous puzzle. He cut a breach in the wall of plausibility; the breach through which many others followed him, each in his own way: Fellini, Márquez, Fuentes, Rushdie. And others, others.

To hell with Saint Garta! His castrating shadow has blocked our view of one of the novel's greatest poets of all time.

PART THREE

*Improvisation in Homage
to Stravinsky*

The Call of the Past

In a 1931 radio lecture, Schoenberg speaks of his masters: *"in erster Linie Bach und Mozart; in zweiter Beethoven, Wagner, Brahms,"*—"in the first place, Bach and Mozart; in the second, Beethoven, Wagner, Brahms." In concise, aphoristic remarks, he goes on to specify what he learned from each of these five composers.

Between the Bach reference and the others there is a very great difference: in Mozart, for example, he learns about "the art of unequal phrase lengths" or "the art of creating secondary ideas," that is to say an utterly individual skill that belongs to Mozart alone. In Bach, he discovers principles that had also operated in all the music for centuries before Bach: first, "the art of inventing groups of notes such that they provide their own accompaniment"; and second, "the art of creating the whole from a single kernel"—*"die Kunst, alles aus einem zu erzeugen."*

These two sentences summarizing the lesson Schoenberg drew from Bach (and from his predecessors) can be taken to describe the whole twelve-tone revolution: in contrast to Classical music and Romantic music, which are built on the alternation of differing musical themes occurring one after the other, both a Bach fugue and a twelve-tone composition, from beginning to end, develop from a single kernel, which is both melody and accompaniment.

Twenty-three years later, when Roland Manuel asks Stravinsky: "What are your major interests these days?" the latter responds: Guillaume de Machaut, Heinrich Isaak, Dufay, Pérotin, and Webern." It is the first time a composer proclaims so firmly the immense importance of the music of the twelfth, the fourteenth, and the fifteenth centuries, and relates it to modern music (to Webern's).

Some years after that, Glenn Gould gives a concert in Moscow for the students of the conservatory; after playing Webern, Schoenberg, and Krenek, he gives his audience a short commentary, saying: "The greatest compliment I can give this music is to say that the principles to be found in it are not new, that they are at least five hundred years old"; then he goes on to play three Bach fugues. It was a carefully considered provocation: socialist realism, then the official doctrine in Russia, was battling modernism in the name of traditional music; Glenn Gould meant to show that the roots of modern music (forbidden in Communist Russia) go much deeper than those of the official music of socialist realism (which was actually nothing but an artificial preservation of romanticism in music).

The Two Halves

The history of European music covers about a thousand years (if I take as its beginnings the first experiments in primitive polyphony). The history of the European novel (if I take as its start the works of Rabelais and Cervantes) covers about four centuries. When I consider these two histories, I cannot shake the sense that they developed in rhythms resembling, so to speak, the two halves of a soccer game. The caesuras, or halftime breaks, in the history of music and in that of the novel do not coincide. In the history of music, the break stretches over a big part of the eighteenth century (the symbolic apogee of the first half occurring in Bach's *The Art of Fugue*, and the start of the second half in the works of the earliest Classical composers); the break in the history of the novel comes a little later: between the eighteenth and the nineteenth centuries—that is, between Laclos and Sterne on the one side and, on the other, Scott and Balzac. This asynchronism shows that the deepest causes governing the rhythm of the history of the arts are not sociological or political but aesthetic: bound up with the intrinsic nature of one art or another; as if the art of the novel, for instance, contained two different potentialities (two different ways of being a novel) that could not be worked out at the same time, in parallel, but could be worked out only successively, one after the other.

The metaphor of the two halves of a game came to me some time ago in the course of a conversation with a friend and does not claim to be at all scholarly; it is an ordinary, elementary observation, naïvely obvious:

when it comes to music and the novel, we are all of us
raised in the aesthetic of the second half. A mass by
Ockeghem or Bach's *The Art of Fugue* are for the average music lover as difficult to comprehend as Webern's
music. However enchanting their stories, the novels of
the eighteenth century intimidate the reader by their
form, to the point where they are much better known
in movie adaptations (which necessarily denature both
their spirit and their form) than through their written
texts. The works of the eighteenth century's most
famous novelist, Samuel Richardson, cannot be found
in bookstores and are practically forgotten. Balzac, on
the contrary, even though he may seem old-fashioned,
is still easy to read; his form is comprehensible, familiar to the reader, and even more important, it is for
that reader the very model of the novel form.

The chasm between the aesthetics of these two
halves makes for a multitude of misunderstandings.
Vladimir Nabokov, in his book on Cervantes, gives a
provocatively negative opinion of *Don Quixote*: over-
valued, naïve, repetitive, and full of unbearable and
implausible cruelty; that "hideous cruelty" makes this
book "one of the most bitter and barbarous ever
penned"; poor Sancho, moving along from one drub-
bing to another, loses all his teeth at least five times.
Yes, Nabokov is right: Sancho loses too many teeth,
but we are not in the world of Zola, where some cruel
act, described precisely and in detail, becomes the
accurate document of a social reality; with Cervantes,
we are in a world created by the magic spells of the
storyteller who invents, who exaggerates, and who is
carried away by his fantasies, his excesses; Sancho's

three hundred broken teeth cannot be taken literally, no more than anything else in this novel. "Madame, a steamroller has just run over your daughter!" "Yes, yes, I'm in the bathtub. Slide her to me under the door." Must we bring charges of cruelty against that old Czech joke from my childhood? Cervantes' great founding work was alive with the spirit of the nonserious, a spirit that was later made incomprehensible by the Romantic aesthetic of the second half, by its demand for plausibility.

The second half not only eclipsed the first, it *repressed* it; the first half has become the bad conscience of the novel and especially of music. Bach's work is the best-known example: Bach's renown during his lifetime; Bach forgotten after his death (forgotten for half a century); the slow rediscovery of Bach over the length of the nineteenth century. Beethoven alone almost succeeded toward the end of his life (that is, seventy years after Bach's death) in integrating Bach's experience into the new aesthetic of music (his repeated efforts to insert fugue into the sonata), whereas after Beethoven, the more the Romantics worshiped Bach, the further they moved away from him in their structural thinking. To make him more accessible they subjectivized and sentimentalized him (Busoni's famous arrangements); then, reacting against that romanticization, came a desire to recover his music as it was played in its own time, which gave rise to some notably insipid performances. It seems to me that, having once passed through the desert of oblivion, Bach's music still keeps its face half veiled.

History as a Landscape Emerging from the Mists

Rather than discuss the forgetting of Bach, I could turn my idea around and say: Bach is the first great composer who, by the enormous weight of his work, compelled the audience to pay attention to his music even though it already belonged to the past. An unprecedented phenomenon, because until the nineteenth century, people lived almost exclusively with contemporary music. They had no living contact with the musical past: even if musicians had studied the music of previous times (and this was rare), they were not in the habit of performing it in public. During the nineteenth century, music of the past began to be revived and played alongside contemporary music and to take on an ever greater presence, to the point that in the twentieth century the balance between the present and the past was reversed: audiences heard the music of earlier times much more than they did contemporary music, and now the latter has virtually disappeared from concert halls.

Bach was thus the first composer to establish his place in the memory of later generations; with him, nineteenth-century Europe not only discovered an important part of music's past, it also discovered music *history*. Europe saw that Bach was not just any past but rather a past that was radically different from the present; thus musical time was revealed abruptly (and for the first time) not just as a series of works but as a series of changes, of eras, of varying aesthetics.

I often imagine him in the year of his death, in the

exact middle of the eighteenth century, bending with clouding eyes over *The Art of Fugue*, a composition whose aesthetic orientation represents the most archaic tendency in Bach's oeuvre (which contains many orientations), a tendency alien to its time, which had already turned completely away from polyphony toward a simple, even simplistic, style that often verged on frivolity or laziness.

The historical position of Bach's work therefore reveals what later generations had begun to forget—that history is not necessarily a path climbing upward (toward the richer, the more cultivated), that the demands of art may be counter to the demands of the moment (of this or that modernity), and that the new (the unique, the inimitable, the previously unsaid) might lie in some direction other than the one everybody sees as progress. Indeed, the future that Bach could discern in the art of his contemporaries and of his juniors must to his eyes have seemed a collapse. When, toward the end of his life, he concentrated exclusively on pure polyphony, he was turning his back on the tastes of his time and on his own composer sons; it was a gesture of defiance against history, a tacit rejection of the future. Bach: an extraordinary crossroads of the historical trends and issues of music. Some hundred years before him, another such crossroads occurs in the work of Monteverdi: this is the meeting ground of two opposing aesthetics (Monteverdi calls them *prima* and *seconda prattica*, the one based on erudite polyphony, the other, programmatically expressive, on monody), and it thus prefigures the move from the first to the second half.

Another extraordinary crossroads of historical

trends: the work of Stravinsky. Music's thousand-year history, which over the course of the nineteenth century was slowly emerging from the mists of oblivion, suddenly toward the middle of our own century (two hundred years after Bach's death) stood revealed in its full breadth like a landscape drenched in light; a unique moment when the whole history of music is totally present, totally accessible and available (thanks to historical research, to radio, to recordings), totally open to the examination of its meaning; this moment of vast reappraisal seems to find its monument in the music of Stravinsky.

The Tribunal of the Feelings

Music is "powerless to express anything at all: a feeling, an attitude, a psychological state," says Stravinsky in *Chronicle of My Life* (1935). This assertion (surely exaggerated, for how can one deny music's ability to arouse feelings?) is elaborated and refined a few lines later: music's *raison d'être*, says Stravinsky, does not reside in its capacity to express feelings. It is curious to note what irritation this attitude provoked.

The conviction, contrary to Stravinsky's, that music's raison d'être is the expression of feelings probably existed always, but it became dominant, widely accepted and self-evident, in the eighteenth century; Jean-Jacques Rousseau states it with a blunt simplicity: like any other art, music imitates the real world, but in a specific way: it "will not represent things directly, but it will arouse in the soul the same impulses that we feel at seeing them." That requires a certain structure in the musical work; Rousseau: "All of music can be composed of only these three things: melody or song, harmony or accompaniment, movement or tempo." I emphasize: harmony *or* accompaniment; that means everything else is subordinate to melody: it is melody that is primordial, and harmony is merely accompaniment, "having very little power over the human heart."

The doctrine of socialist realism, which two centuries later was to muzzle Russian music for over half a century, asserted this same thing. "Formalist" composers were berated for neglecting melody (the chief ideologue, Zhdanov, was indignant because their music could not be whistled on the way out of the concert); they were exhorted to express "the whole range of human feelings" (modern music, from Debussy on, was denounced for its inability to do so); music's faculty for expressing the feelings reality arouses in man gave it "realism" (just as Rousseau said). (Socialist realism in music: the principles of the second half transformed into dogmas to block modernism.)

The most severe and thorough criticism of Stravinsky is surely Theodor Adorno's in his famous book *The Philosophy of Modern Music* (1949). Adorno depicts the situation in music as if it were a political battlefield: Schoenberg the positive hero, the representative of progress (though a progress that might be termed tragic, at a time when progress is over), and Stravinsky the negative hero, the representative of restoration. The Stravinskian refusal to see subjective confession as music's raison d'être becomes one target of the Adorno critique; this "antipsychological furor" is, he says, a form of "indifference toward the world";

Stravinsky's desire to objectivize music is a kind of tacit accord with the capitalist society that crushes human subjectivity; for it is the "liquidation of the individual that Stravinsky's music celebrates," nothing less.

Ernest Ansermet, an excellent musician and conductor, and one of the foremost performers of Stravinsky's work ("one of my most faithful and devoted friends," says Stravinsky in *Chronicle of My Life*), later became his implacable critic; his objections are fundamental, they are concerned with "music's raison d'être." Ansermet says it is "the affective activity latent in men's hearts . . . that has always been the source of music"; the "ethical essence" of music lies in the expression of that "affective activity"; with Stravinsky, who "refuses to invest his person in the act of musical expression," music "thereby ceases to be an aesthetic expression of the human ethic"; thus, for instance, "his *Mass* is not the expression of the mass but its *portrayal*, which might just as well have been written by an irreligious musician" and which, consequently, provides only a "ready-made religiosity"; by thus undercutting the true raison d'être of music (by substituting portrayals for religious avowal), Stravinsky fails in nothing less than his ethical obligation.

Why this fury? Is it the legacy of the previous century, the romanticism in us striking out at its most significant, its most thorough negation? Has Stravinsky violated some existential need hidden within us all? The need to consider damp eyes better than dry eyes, the hand on the heart better than the hand in the pocket, belief better than skepticism, passion better than serenity, faith better than knowledge?

Ansermet proceeds from criticism of the music to criticism of its author: if Stravinsky "neither made nor tried to make his music an act of self-expression, it's not out of free choice, but out of a kind of limitation in his nature, a lack of autonomy in his affective activity (not to speak of his poverty of heart, a heart that will stay poor until it has something to love)."

Damn! What did Ansermet, that most faithful friend, know about Stravinsky's poverty of heart? What did he, that most devoted friend, know about Stravinsky's capacity to love? And where did he get his utter certainty that the heart is ethically superior to the brain? Are not vile acts committed as often with the heart's help as without it? Can't fanatics, with their bloody hands, boast of a high degree of "affective activity"? Will we ever be done with this imbecile sentimental Inquisition, the heart's Reign of Terror?

What Is Superficial and What Is Profound?

The soldiers of the heart assail Stravinsky, or else, in an effort to salvage his music, they try to disconnect it from its author's "erroneous" ideas. That noble determination to "salvage" the music of composers who might have too little heart occurs quite often with regard to the musicians of the first half. By chance, I came upon a little commentary by a French musicologist; it concerns Rabelais's great contemporary Clément Janequin and his so-called descriptive works, like *"Le Chant des oiseaux"* ("Birdsong") or *"Le Caquet des femmes"* ("Women's Chatter") (the italics in the following are mine): . . ." "Nonetheless, these pieces remain rather *superficial.* Now, Janequin is a far more complete artist than people are willing to admit, for aside from his undeniable *pictorial gifts,* his work displays *a tender poetry, a penetrating ardor in the expression of feelings.* . . . This is a poet of subtlety, sensitive to nature's beauties; he is also *a peerless bard of womankind,* to whose praise he brings *tones of tenderness, admiration, respect.* . . ."

Note the vocabulary: the poles of good and evil are designated by the adjective "superficial" and its understood contrary, "profound." But are Janequin's "descriptive" compositions actually superficial? In these few works, Janequin transcribes nonmusical sounds (birdsong, women's chatter, the racket of the streets, the sounds of a hunt or a battle, and so on) by musical means (choral singing); that "description" is worked out polyphonically. The union of "naturalistic" imitation (which provides Janequin with some wonderful new sonorities) and erudite polyphony, a union, that is, of two nearly incompatible extremes, is fascinating: this is an art that is elegant, playful, joyous, and full of humor.

And yet: it is precisely the words "elegant," "playful," "joyous," "humor," that sentimental rhetoric sets in opposition to the profound. But what is profound and what is superficial? For Janequin's critic, superficial are the "pictorial gifts" and "description"; profound are the "penetrating ardor in the expression of feelings" and the "tones of tenderness, admiration, respect" for womankind. Thus "profound" is what touches on the feelings. But one could define "the profound" in another way: profound is what touches on the essential. The problem Janequin touches on in his compositions is the fundamental ontological problem of music: the problem of the relation between noise and musical sound.

Music and Noise

When man created a musical sound (by singing or by playing an instrument), he divided the acoustical world into two sharply distinct parts: that of artificial sounds and that of natural sounds. In his music, Janequin sought to put them together. In the middle of the sixteenth century, he thus prefigured what in the twentieth century would be done by, for instance, Janacek (his studies of spoken language), Bartók, or, in an extremely systematic way, Messiaen (in the works inspired by birdsong).

Janequin's art reminds us that there exists an acoustic universe outside the human soul, one that consists not merely of nature sounds but also of human voices speaking, singing, and giving sonic flesh to everyday life as well as to festive occasions. He reminds us that the composer can give a great musical form to that "objective" universe.

One of Janacek's most original compositions: *The Seventy Thousand* (1909): a piece for men's chorus about the fate of the Silesian miners. The second half of the work (which should be in every anthology of modern music) is an explosion of shouts from the crowd, shouts that tangle together in a fascinating tumult: a composition that (despite its amazing dramatic emotional charge) comes curiously close to the madrigals that, in Janequin's time, turned the street cries of Paris and London into music.

I think of Stravinsky's *Les Noces* (written between 1914 and 1923): a *portrayal* (the term Ansermet uses as a pejorative is actually quite appropriate) of a village wedding; we hear songs, noises, speeches, shouts, calls, monologues, joking (a tumult of voices prefigured by Janacek), accompanied by an orchestration (four pianos and percussion) of fascinating harshness (which prefigures Bartók).

And I think of Bartók's piano suite *Out of Doors* (1926), the fourth part: nature sounds (the voices of frogs at a pond, it seems to me) suggest to Bartók rare and strange melodic motifs; then into these animal tones merges a folk song that, human invention though it is, lies on the same plane as the frog sounds; it is not a lied, that song of the Romantics meant to display the "affective activity" of the composer's soul; it is a melody come from the outside as a noise among other noises.

And I think, too, of the *Adagio* of Bartók's Third Piano Concerto (a work of his last, his sad, American period). The hypersubjective theme, ineffably melancholy, alternates with a second, this one hyperobjective (which incidentally recalls the fourth part of the *Out of Doors* suite): as if a soul's sorrow could find consolation only in the nonsentience of nature.

I say, indeed: "consolation in the nonsentience of nature." For nonsentience is consoling; the world of nonsentience is the world outside human life; it is eternity; "it is the sea gone off with the sun" (Rimbaud). I remember the gloomy years I spent in Bohemia early in the Russian occupation. I fell in love

then with Varèse and Xenakis: those pictures of
sound-worlds that were objective but nonexistent
spoke to me of a life freed of human subjectivity,
aggressive and burdensome; they spoke of the sweetly
nonhuman beauty of the world before or after
mankind moved through it.

Melody

I listen to a polyphonic chant for two voices from the
twelfth-century School of Notre-Dame in Paris: under-
neath, in augmented note values, as a *cantus firmus*,
an ancient Gregorian chant (a chant that goes back to
an immemorial and probably non-European past);
above it, in shorter note values, unfolds the polyphonic
accompaniment's melody. This embrace of two
melodies belonging to two different eras (centuries
apart) has something marvelous about it: like reality
and parable at once, here is the birth of European
music as art: a melody is created to go in counterpoint
with another, very old, melody whose origins are
almost unknown; so this new one is there as something
secondary, subordinate, it is there to *serve*; though
"secondary," it is this voice that brings to bear all the
invention, all the labor, of the medieval musician,
whereas the melody it accompanies has been taken
unchanged from an antique repertoire.

This old polyphonic composition delights me: the
new melody on top is long, unending, and *unmemorizable*; it is not the product of some *sudden inspiration*,
it did not spring forth as the direct expression of some
state of mind; it has the quality of an *elaboration*, a

"craftsman's" work of ornamentation, a work done not to let the artist open his soul (show his "affective activity," to use Ansermet's term) but to let him, in all humility, embellish a liturgy.

And it's my impression that until Bach the art of melody would keep that quality the earliest polyphonic composers gave it. I listen to the Adagio of Bach's E Major Violin Concerto: like a kind of *cantus firmus*, the orchestra (the bass instruments) plays a very simple theme, readily memorizable and many times repeated, while the violin melody (the focus of the composer's melodic challenge) soars above, incomparably longer, more various, richer than the orchestra's *cantus firmus* (to which it is nonetheless subordinate), beautiful, spellbinding yet elusive, unmemorizable, and for us children of the second half, sublimely archaic.

The situation changes with the dawn of the Classical. Composition loses its polyphonic nature; in the sonority of the accompaniment harmonies, the autonomy of the various singular voices disappears, and disappears still more as the great innovation of the second half—the symphonic orchestra with its thickness of sound—gains prominence; the melody that was "secondary," "subordinate," becomes the main point in composition and dominates musical structure, which incidentally undergoes a complete transformation.

Then the character of melody changes too: no more is it the long line that runs through an entire piece; it can be reduced to a phrase of a few measures, a phrase that is very expressive and concentrated, and thus easily memorizable, that can catch (or provoke) a direct emotion (more than ever before, music is set a great semantic task: to capture and musically "describe" all the emotions and their nuances). This is why the present-day audience applies the term "great melodist" to the composers of the second half—to a Mozart, a Chopin—but rarely to Bach or Vivaldi and still less to Josquin des Prés or Palestrina: the current idea of melody (of what constitutes beautiful melody) was shaped by the Classical aesthetic.

Yet it is not true that Bach is less melodic than Mozart; it is only that his melody is different. *The Art of Fugue*: the famous theme

is that kernel out of which (as Schoenberg said) the whole is created; but that is not the melodic treasure of *The Art of Fugue*; the treasure is in all the melodies that arise from this theme and form the counterpoint to it. I like very much Hermann Scherchen's orchestration and recorded interpretation; for example, Contrapunctus IV, the *fourth single fugue*: he conducts it at half the customary speed (Bach did not prescribe the tempi); immediately, at that slow tempo, the whole of its unsuspected melodic beauty is revealed. That *remelodization* of Bach has nothing to do with *romanticization* (no rubato, no added chords in Scherchen); what I hear is the authentic melody of the first half, elusive, unmemorizable, irreducible to a brief phrase, a melody (an entwining of melodies) that bewitches me by its ineffable serenity. Impossible to hear it without great emotion. But it is an emotion essentially different from one stirred by a Chopin nocturne.

As if, behind the art of melody, there hid two possible intentionalities, contrary to one another: as if a Bach fugue, by bringing us to contemplate a beauty of being that is outside the subjective, aimed to make us forget our moods, our passions and pains, ourselves; and as if on the other hand Romantic melody aimed to make us plunge into ourselves, feel the self with a terrible intensity, and forget everything outside.

Modernism's Great Works as Rehabilitation of the First Half

The great novelists of the post-Proust period—I have especially in mind Kafka, Musil, Broch, Gombrowicz, or, in my generation, Fuentes—were highly sensitive to the nearly forgotten aesthetic of the novel previous to the nineteenth century: they incorporated essayistic reflection into the art of the novel; made composition freer; reclaimed the right to digression; breathed the spirit of the nonserious and of play into the novel; repudiated the dogmas of psychological realism in creating characters without trying to compete (like Balzac) with the *état civil*—with the state registry of citizens; and above all: they refused any obligation to give the reader the illusion of reality: an obligation that reigned supreme throughout the novel's second half.

The point of this rehabilitation of the first-half novelistic principles is not a return to this or that retro style; nor is it a simpleminded rejection of the nineteenth-century novel; the point of the rehabilitation is more general: to *redefine* and *broaden* the very notion of the novel; to resist the *reduction* worked by the nineteenth century's aesthetic of the novel; to give the novel its *entire* historical experience for a grounding.

I do not mean to draw a facile parallel between the novel and music, the structural issues of the two arts not being comparable; but the historical situations are similar: like the great novelists, the great modern composers (Stravinsky and Schoenberg both) determined to encompass *all* the centuries of music, to rethink and remake the scale of values of its *whole* history; to do this, they had to extricate music from the rut of the second half (by the way: the term "neoclassicism" commonly pinned on Stravinsky is misleading, for his most decisive excursions into the past reach into eras earlier than the Classical); from which comes their reticence: as to composition techniques originating with the sonata; as to the preeminence of melody; as to the sonic demagogy of symphonic orchestration; but from which comes, above all: their refusal to see music's raison d'être *exclusively* as an avowal of emotional life, an attitude that during the nineteenth century became as coercive as did the requirement of plausibility for the novel.

Although that inclination to reread and reevaluate the entire history of music is common to all the great modernists (if it is, as I believe, the mark that distinguishes great modern art from modernist trumpery), still, it is Stravinsky who expresses it more clearly than anyone else (and hyperbolically, I would add). That, by the way, is the focus of his detractors' attacks: in his effort to root himself in the whole history of music they see eclecticism; a lack of originality; a failure of invention. His "incredible diversity of stylistic procedures . . . amounts to an absence of style," says Ansermet. And

Adorno, sarcastically: Stravinsky's music is inspired only by music, it is "music made from music."

Unfair judgments: for while Stravinsky, like no other composer before or after him, did turn for inspiration to the whole span of music, in no way does that lessen the originality of his art. And I do not merely mean that the same personal traits are always visible beneath the shifts in his style. I mean that it is precisely his vagabondage through musical history—his conscious, purposeful "eclecticism," gigantic and unmatched—that is his total and incomparable originality.

The "Third Half" or Third Period

But what is the significance, in Stravinsky, of this determination to encompass the whole span of music? What is the point?

As a young man, I would answer without hesitation: to me, Stravinsky was one of those figures who had opened the doors onto distances I saw as boundless. I thought he meant to summon up and mobilize all the powers, all the means available to the history of music, for the *infinite journey that is modern art*.

The infinite journey that is modern art? Since then, I've lost that feeling. The journey was a short one. That is why, for my metaphor of the two game halves of music history, I've imagined modern music as a mere postlude, an epilogue to the history of music, a celebration that marks the end of the adventure, a sky ablaze at the end of the day.

Now I do hesitate: even though it is true that the time of modern music has been so short, even though it has lasted only a generation or two, and has thus really been no more than an epilogue, still, by reason of its enormous beauty, its artistic importance, its entirely new aesthetic, does it not deserve to be considered an era complete unto itself, a *"third half" or third period*? Should I not revise my metaphor about the histories of music and of the novel? Should I not say that they happened over three periods?

Yes, I do revise my metaphor, and all the more willingly as I am deeply, passionately fond of that third period, that "sky ablaze at the end of the day," fond of that period which I believe I myself am part of, even if I am part of something that is already finished.

But to return to my question: what is the significance of Stravinsky's determination to encompass the whole span of music? What is the point?

An image hounds me: according to a popular belief, at the moment of his death a person sees his whole life pass before his eyes. In Stravinsky's work, European music recalled its thousand-year history; that was its final dream before setting out for an eternal dreamless sleep.

Playful Transcription

Let us distinguish two things: on the one hand: the general trend for restoring forgotten principles of music of the past, a trend that runs through all Stravinsky's work and that of his great contemporaries; on the other hand: the direct dialogue that Stravinsky carries on with Tchaikovsky, then with Pergolesi, then with Gesualdo, and so on; these "direct dialogues," transcriptions of this or that old work, in this or that particular style, are a procedure of Stravinsky's own that we find in practically no other of his composer contemporaries (we do find it in Picasso).

Adorno interprets Stravinsky's transcriptions thus (I emphasize the key terms): "These notes"—the dissonant notes, alien to the harmony, which Stravinsky uses in *Pulcinella*, for instance—"become the marks of the *violence* the composer wreaks against the idiom, and it is that *violence* we relish about them, that *battering, that violation, so to speak, of musical life*. Though dissonance may originally have been the expression of *subjective suffering*, its harshness shifts in value and becomes the sign of a *social constraint*, whose agent is the style-setting composer. His works have no other material but the emblems of that *constraint*, a necessity external to the subject, having nothing in common with it, and which is merely imposed from the outside. It may be that the widespread effect of these works of Stravinsky's is due in large part to the fact that inadvertently, and under color of aestheticism, *they in their own way trained men to something that was soon methodically inflicted on them at the political level.*"

Let us recapitulate: a dissonance is justified if it expresses "subjective suffering," but in Stravinsky (who is morally guilty, as we know, of never discussing his sufferings) that very dissonance is the sign of brutality; a parallel is drawn (by a brilliant short circuit of Adorno thought) with political brutality: thus the dissonant chords added to Pergolesi's music prefigure (and thereby prepare) the coming political oppression (which in this particular historical context can mean only one thing: fascism).

I had my own experience with the free transcription of a work from the past when, early in the 1970s, while I was still in Prague, I set about writing a variation for the theater on *Jacques le Fataliste*. Diderot being for me the embodiment of a free, rational, critical mind, I experienced my affection for him at the time as a kind of yearning for the West (to my eyes, the Russian occupation of my country represented a forced de-Westernization). But the meaning of things keeps changing: today I would say that Diderot embodied for me the first half of the art of the novel and that my play celebrated various principles well known to the novelists of old, and dear to me as well: (1) the euphoric freedom of composition; (2) the constant association of libertine stories and philosophical reflections; (3) the nonserious, ironical, parodic, shocking nature of those reflections. The rules of the game were clear: what I did was not an *adaptation* of Diderot, it was my own play, my *variation* on Diderot, my homage to Diderot: I completely rewrote his novel; the love stories are taken from him, but the ideas in the dialogue are largely mine; anyone can instantly see lines in it that are unthinkable from Diderot's pen; the eighteenth century was optimistic, my time is not, I myself still less so, and in my play the Master and Jacques characters indulge in dark excesses barely imaginable in the age of Enlightenment.

After that little experience of my own I can only call stupid those remarks on Stravinsky's brutality and violence. He loved his old master as I loved mine. In adding twentieth-century dissonances to melodies of the eighteenth, perhaps he imagined he might intrigue his master out in the beyond, that he might tell him something important about our time, that he might even amuse him. He needed to address him, to talk to him. The *playful transcription* of an old work was for him like a way of establishing communication between centuries.

Playful Transcription According to Kafka

A curious novel, Kafka's *Amerika*: indeed, why should this young twenty-nine-year-old writer have laid his first novel in a continent where he had never set foot? This choice shows a clear intent: to not do realism; better yet: to not do a serious work. He did not even try to palliate his ignorance by research; he invented his idea of America from second-rate readings, from popular prints, and indeed, the novel's image of America is (intentionally) made up of clichés; the main inspiration for the characters and plot (as he acknowledged in his diary) is Dickens, especially *David Copperfield* (Kafka describes the first chapter of *Amerika* as "a sheer imitation of Dickens"): he picks up particular motifs from it (and lists them: "the story of the trunk, the boy who delights and charms everyone, the menial labor, the sweetheart in the country house, the filthy living quarters"), and he draws on its characters (Karl is an affectionate parody of David Copperfield) and especially on the atmosphere that all Dickens's novels bathe in: the sentimentality, the naïve distinction between good and evil figures. Adorno speaks of Stravinsky's music as a "music made from music"; Kafka's *Amerika* is a "literature made from literature," and within the genre it is even a classic work, perhaps a seminal one.

The first page of the novel: in the port of New York, Karl is about to leave the ship when he realizes that he has forgotten his umbrella below. In order to go back for it, with a gullibility that is barely believable he entrusts his steamer trunk (a heavy trunk holding everything he owns) to a stranger: of course, he loses the trunk and the umbrella both. From the first lines, the spirit of playful parody generates an imaginary world where nothing is completely plausible and everything is a little comical.

Kafka's castle, which exists on no map anywhere, is no more unreal than that America conceived as a cliché picture of the new civilization of gigantism and the machine. In the house of his uncle the senator, Karl comes across a desk that is an extraordinarily complicated machine, with a hundred compartments keyed to a hundred push buttons, an object at once practical and utterly useless, at once technical wonder and nonsense. I counted ten such devices in the novel, all marvelous, entertaining, and implausible, from the uncle's desk, the mazelike country house, the Hotel Occidental (monstrously complex architecture, diabolically bureaucratic organization), to the Oklahoma Theater, itself another enormous, incomprehensible administration. So it is through parodic playing (playing with clichés) that Kafka first set out his greatest theme, that of the labyrinthine social organization where man loses his way and proceeds to his ruin. (Genetically speaking: the comical mechanism of the uncle's desk is the ancestor of the terrifying castle administration.) Kafka managed to capture this theme, grave as it is, not by means of a realistic novel, grounded in some Zolaesque examination of society, but by just that seemingly frivolous means of "literature made from literature" which allowed his imagination all the freedom it required (freedom for exaggerations, for enormities, for improbabilities, freedom for playful inventions).

Heartlessness Masked by a Style Overflowing with Feeling

In *Amerika*, there are many unaccountably excessive sentimental gestures. The end of the first chapter: Karl is already set to go off with his uncle, the stoker is staying behind, abandoned in the captain's cabin. Then Karl (I stress the key phrases) "went over to the stoker, pulled the man's right hand out of his belt and *held it lightly in his.* . . . Karl *drew his fingers back and forth between the stoker's*, while the stoker looked around with shining eyes, *as if blessed by a great happiness, but one that nobody could grudge him.*

"'Now you must get ready to defend yourself, answer yes and no, or else these people won't have any idea of the truth. You must promise me to do what I tell you, for I'm afraid, and I've good reason for it, that I won't be able to help you anymore.' And then Karl *burst out crying and kissed the stoker's hand*, taking that seamed, almost nerveless hand and *pressing it to his cheek like a treasure* that he would soon have to give up. But now his uncle the senator was at his side and *with only the slightest compulsion* led him away."

Another example: At the end of the evening at Pollunder's country house, Karl explains at length why he wants to go back to his uncle's. "During this long speech of Karl's, Mr. Pollunder had listened attentively, often, particularly when Uncle Jacob was mentioned . . . *pressing Karl to himself. . . .*"

The sentimental gestures of the characters are not only exaggerated, they are inappropriate. Karl has known the stoker for barely an hour and has no reason to be so passionately attached to him. And if we decide that the young man is naïvely touched by the prospect of a manly friendship, we are all the more amazed when, a moment later, he so readily lets himself be carried off from his new friend, without any resistance.

In that evening scene, Pollunder knows full well that the uncle has already thrown Karl out of his house; that is why he takes Karl in an affectionate embrace. Yet when, in Pollunder's presence, Karl reads the uncle's letter and learns of his own sad fate, Pollunder shows him no further affection and offers him no help.

In Kafka's *Amerika*, we find ourselves in a universe of feelings that are inappropriate, misplaced, exaggerated, unfathomable, or—the reverse—bizarrely missing. In his diary, Kafka characterized Dickens's novels by the words: "Heartlessness masked by a style overflowing with feeling." Such is the real meaning of that theater of showily displayed and instantly forgotten feelings that is Kafka's novel. This "critique of sentimentality" (an implicit, parodic, droll, never aggressive critique) is aimed not at Dickens alone but at romanticism generally, at its heirs, Kafka's contemporaries, particularly the expressionists, with their cult of hysteria and madness; it is aimed at the entire Holy Church of the Heart; and once more, it brings together those two apparently very different artists, Kafka and Stravinsky.

A Little Boy in Ecstasy

Of course, one cannot say that music (all music) is incapable of expressing feelings; the music of the Romantic era is authentically and legitimately expressive; but even about that music it can be said: its *worth* has nothing to do with the intensity of the feelings it provokes. For music can powerfully stir feelings with no musical *art* at all. I recall my childhood: sitting at the piano, I would throw myself into passionate improvisations for which I needed nothing but a C-minor chord and the subdominant F minor, played *fortissimo* over and over again. The two chords and the endlessly repeated primitive melodic motif made me experience an emotion more intense than any Chopin, any Beethoven, has ever given me. (One time my musician father, completely furious—I never saw him so furious before or after—rushed into the room, lifted me off the piano stool, and with a disgust he could barely control, carried me into the dining room and set me down under the table.)

What I was experiencing during those improvisations was an *ecstasy*. What is ecstasy? The boy banging on the keyboard feels an enthusiasm (or a sorrow, or a delight), and the emotion rises to such a pitch of intensity that it becomes unbearable: the boy flees into a state of blindness and deafness where everything is forgotten, even oneself. Through ecstasy, emotion reaches its climax, and thereby at the same time its negation (its oblivion).

Ecstasy means being "outside oneself," as indicated by the etymology of the Greek word: the act of leaving one's position (*stasis*). To be "outside oneself" does not mean outside the present moment, like a dreamer escaping into the past or the future. Just the opposite: ecstasy is absolute identity with the present instant, total forgetting of past and future. If we obliterate the future and the past, the present moment stands in empty space, outside life and its chronology, outside time and independent of it (this is why it can be likened to eternity, which too is the negation of time).

We can see the acoustical image of emotion in the Romantic melody of a lied: its length seems intended for sustaining emotion, building it, causing its slow enjoyment. Ecstasy, on the other hand, cannot be mirrored in a melody, because memory strangled by ecstasy is incapable of retaining the sequence of notes in a melodic phrase, however short; the acoustical image of ecstasy is the cry (or: a very brief melodic motif that imitates a cry).

The classic example of ecstasy is the moment of orgasm. Think back to the time before women had the benefit of the pill. It often happened that at the moment of climax a lover forgot to slide out of his mistress's body and made her a mother, even though, a few moments earlier, he had firmly intended to be extremely careful. That second of ecstasy made him forget both his determination (his immediate past) and his interest (his future).

The instant of ecstasy thus weighed more heavily on the scales than the unwanted child; and since the unwanted child will probably fill the lover's whole life span with his unwanted presence, it may be said that one instant of ecstasy weighed more than a whole lifetime. The lover's lifetime faced the instant of ecstasy from roughly the same inferior status as the finite has facing eternity. Man desires eternity, but all he can get is its imitation: the instant of ecstasy.

I recall a day in my youth: I was with a friend in his car; people were crossing the street in front of us. I saw a person I disliked and pointed him out to my friend: "Run him over!" It was of course only a verbal joke, but my friend was in a state of great euphoria, and he hit the accelerator. The man took fright, slipped, fell. My friend stopped the car just in time. The man was not hurt, but people crowded around and threatened (understandably) to lynch us. Yet my friend was not a murderer by nature. My words had sent him into a momentary ecstasy (actually, one of the oddest: the ecstasy of a joke).

We are used to connecting the notion of ecstasy to great mystical moments. But there is such a thing as everyday, ordinary, vulgar ecstasy: the ecstasy of anger, the ecstasy of speed at the wheel, the ecstasy of ear-splitting noise, ecstasy in the soccer stadium. Living is a perpetual heavy effort not to lose sight of ourselves, to stay solidly present in ourselves, in our *stasis*. Step outside ourselves for a mere instant, and we verge on death's dominion.

Delight and Ecstasy

I wonder if Adorno ever found the slightest pleasure in listening to Stravinsky's music. Pleasure? By his lights, Stravinsky's music offers only one such: "the perverse pleasure of deprivation"; for all it does is "deprive" itself of everything: of expressivity; of orchestral sonority; of developmental technique; casting a "spiteful look" on the old forms, it deforms them; "grimacing," it is incapable of invention, it only "ironizes," "caricatures," "parodies"; it is just "negation," not merely of nineteenth-century music but of music altogether ("Stravinsky's music is a music from which music is banished," says Adorno).

Curious, curious. And what about the delight that beams from that music?

I remember the Picasso exhibition in Prague in the mid-sixties. One painting has stayed with me. A woman and a man are eating watermelon: the woman is seated, the man is lying on the ground, his legs lifted up to the sky in a gesture of unspeakable joy. And the whole thing painted with a delectable offhandedness that made me think the painter, as he painted the picture, must have been feeling the same joy as the man with his legs lifted up.

The delight of the painter painting the man with his legs lifted up is a double delight; it is the delight of contemplating delight (with a smile). It is the smile that interests me. In the delight of the man lifting his legs up to the sky the painter glimpses a wonderful tinge of the comical, and he rejoices in it. His own smile spurs him to a merry, heedless invention, just as heedless as the gesture of the man lifting his legs to the sky. So the delight I'm talking about bears the mark of humor; this is what sets it apart from the delight of other ages in art, from the Romantic delight of Wagner's Tristan, for instance, or from the idyllic delight of a Philemon and Baucis. (Is it a fatal lack of humor that makes Adorno so unreceptive to Stravinsky's music?)

Beethoven wrote the "Ode to Joy," but that Beethovenian joy is a ceremony that requires us to stand at respectful attention. The rondos and minuets of the Classical symphonies are, so to speak, an invitation to the dance, but the delight I'm talking about and that I love would not proclaim itself as delight through the collective act of a dance. This is why no polka makes me happy except Stravinsky's "Circus Polka," which is written not for us to dance to but for us to listen to, with our legs lifted up to the sky.

There are works in modern art that have discovered an inimitable delight in being, the delight that shows in a euphoric recklessness of imagination, in the pleasure of inventing, of surprising—even of shocking—by an invention. One might draw up a whole list of works of art that are suffused with this delight: along with Stravinsky (*Petrushka*, *Les Noces*, *Renard*, the *Capriccio* for Piano and Orchestra, the Violin Concerto, etc., etc.), everything by Miró; Klee's paintings; Dufy's; Dubuffet's; certain Apollinaire writings; late Janacek (*Nursery Rhymes*, Sextet for Wind Instruments, his opera *The Cunning Little Vixen*); some of Milhaud's works; and some of Poulenc's: *Les Mamelles de Tirésias*, his comic opera on a text by Apollinaire, written in the last days of the war, was denounced by people who thought it scandalous to celebrate the Liberation with a piece of fun; and indeed, the age of delight (of that rare delight which humor sets aglow) was over; after the Second World War, only the very old masters Matisse and Picasso still managed, against the spirit of the times, to keep it going in their work.

In this listing of the great works of delight, I cannot overlook jazz music. The whole jazz repertory consists of variations on a relatively small number of melodies. So it is that all throughout jazz we keep catching sight of a smile that has slipped in between the original melody and its elaboration. Like Stravinsky, the great jazz masters enjoyed the art of *playful transcription*, and they composed their own versions not only of old Negro songs but also of Bach, of Mozart, of Chopin; Ellington does transcriptions of Tchaikovsky and Grieg, and for his *Uwis Suite*, he composes a variant of a village polka that recalls *Petrushka* in spirit. The smile is not only invisibly present in the space that separates Ellington from his "portrayal" of Grieg, it is fully visible on the faces of the old Dixieland musicians: come the moment of his solo (which is always partly improvised—that is, always brings a few surprises), the musician steps forward a little, then yields to another musician and gives himself over to the pleasure of listening (the pleasure of other surprises).

At jazz concerts people applaud. To applaud means: I have listened to you carefully and now I am declaring my appreciation. The music called "rock" changes the situation. An important fact: at rock concerts people do not applaud. It would be almost sacrilege to applaud and thus to bring to notice the critical distance between the person playing and the person listening; we come here not to judge and evaluate but to surrender to the music, to scream along with the musicians, to merge with them; we come here to seek identification, not pleasure; effusion, not delight. We go into ecstasy here: the beat is strong and steady, the melodic motifs are short and endlessly repeated, there are no dynamic contrasts, everything is *fortissimo*, the song tends toward the highest range and resembles screaming. Here we're no longer in those little nightspots where the music wraps the couple in intimacy; we're in huge halls, in stadiums, pressed one against the next, and, if we're dancing at a club there are no couples; each person is doing his moves by himself and together with the whole crowd at the same time. The music turns the individuals into a single collective body: talking here about individualism and hedonism is just one of the self-mystifications of our time, which (like any other time, by the way) wants to see itself as different from what it is.

Evil's Scandalous Beauty

What irritates me in Adorno is his short-circuit method that, with a fearsome facility, links works of art to political (sociological) causes, consequences, or meanings; extremely nuanced ideas (Adorno's musicological knowledge is admirable) thereby lead to extremely impoverished conclusions; in fact, given that an era's political tendencies are always reducible to just two opposing tendencies, a work of art necessarily ends up being classified as either progressive or reactionary;

and since reaction is evil, the inquisition can start the trial proceedings.

Le Sacre du printemps: a ballet that ends with the sacrifice of a young girl, who must die for springtime to return. According to Adorno: Stravinsky is on the side of barbarism; his "music does not identify with the victim, but rather with the destructive element." (I wonder: why the verb "identify"? how does Adorno know whether Stravinsky is "identifying" with something or not? why not say "paint," or "portray," "show," "represent"? Answer: because only *identifying* with evil is culpable and can justify a trial.)

I have always, deeply, violently, detested those who look for a *position* (political, philosophical, religious, whatever) in a work of art rather than searching it for an *effort to know*, to understand, to grasp this or that aspect of reality. Until Stravinsky, music was never able to give barbaric rites a grand form. We could not imagine them musically. Which means: we could not imagine the *beauty* of the barbaric. Without its beauty, the barbaric would remain incomprehensible. (I stress this: to know any phenomenon deeply requires understanding its beauty, actual or potential.) Saying that a bloody rite does possess some beauty—there's the scandal, unbearable, unacceptable. And yet, unless we understand this scandal, unless we get to the very bottom of it, we cannot understand much about man. Stravinsky gives the barbaric rite a musical form that is powerful and convincing but does not lie: listen to the last section of the *Sacre*, the *"Danse sacrale"* ("Sacrificial Dance"): it does not dodge the horror. It is there. Merely shown? Not denounced? But if it were denounced—stripped of its beauty, shown in its hideousness—it would be a cheat, a simplification, a piece of "propaganda." It is *because* it is beautiful that the girl's murder is so horrible.

Just as he made a portrayal of the mass and a portrayal of the Shrovetide fair (*Petrushka*), here Stravinsky made a portrayal of barbaric ecstasy. It is all the more interesting in that he had always, and explicitly, declared himself a partisan of the Apollonian principle, an adversary of the Dionysian: *Le Sacre du printemps* (particularly its ritual dances) is the Apollonian portrayal of Dionysian ecstasy: in this portrayal, the ecstatic elements (the aggressively beating rhythm, the few extremely short melodic motifs, many times repeated but never developed, and sounding like shrieks), are transformed into great, refined art (for instance, despite its aggressive quality, the rhythm grows so complex through the rapid alternation of measures with different time signatures that it creates an artificial, unreal, completely stylized beat); still, the Apollonian beauty of this portrayal of barbarity does not obscure its horror; it makes us see that at the very bottom point of the ecstasy there is only the harsh rhythm, the sharp blows of percussion, an extreme numbness, death.

Emigration Arithmetic

The life of an émigré—there's a matter of arithmetic: Jósef Teodor Konrad Korzeniowski (famous under the name Joseph Conrad) lived seventeen years in Poland (and in Russia, with his exiled family), the rest of his life, fifty years, in England (or on English ships). He was thus able to adopt English as his writing language, and English themes as well. Only his allergy to things Russian (ah, poor Gide, incapable of understanding Conrad's puzzling aversion to Dostoyevsky!) preserves a trace of his Polishness.

Bohuslav Martinu lived in Bohemia till he was thirty-two, then for thirty-six years in France, Switzerland, America, and Switzerland again. A nostalgia for the old country always echoed in his work, and he always called himself a Czech composer. Yet after the war, he declined all invitations from back there, and by his express wish, he was buried in Switzerland. Foiling his last will, in 1979, twenty years after his death, agents of the motherland managed to kidnap his corpse and solemnly install it beneath his native soil.

Gombrowicz lived for thirty-five years in Poland, twenty-three in Argentina, six in France. Yet he could write his books only in Polish, and the characters in his novels are Polish. In 1964, during a stay in Berlin, he is invited to Poland. He hesitates, and in the end, he refuses. His body is buried in Vence, in the south of France.

Vladimir Nabokov lived in Russia for twenty years, twenty-one in Europe (in England, Germany, and France), twenty years in America, sixteen in Switzerland. He adopted English as his writing language, but American themes a bit less thoroughly; there are many Russian characters in his novels. Yet he was unequivocal and insistent in proclaiming himself an American citizen and writer. His body lies at Montreux, in Switzerland.

Kazimierz Brandys lived in Poland for sixty-five years, moving to Paris after the Jaruzelski putsch in

1981. He writes only in Polish, on Polish themes, and yet, even though since 1989 there is no longer a political reason to stay abroad, he is not going back to live in Poland (which provides me the pleasure of seeing him from time to time).

This hasty scan reveals, for one thing, an émigré's artistic problem: the numerically equal blocks of a lifetime are unequal in weight, depending on whether they comprise young or adult years. The adult years may be richer and more important for life and for creative activity both, but the subconscious, memory, language, all the understructure of creativity, are formed very early; for a doctor, that won't make problems, but for a novelist or a composer, leaving the place to which his imagination, his obsessions, and thus his fundamental themes are bound could make for a kind of ripping apart. He must mobilize all his powers, all his artist's wiles, to turn the disadvantages of that situation to benefits.

Emigration is hard from the purely personal standpoint as well: people generally think of the pain of nostalgia; but what is worse is the pain of estrangement: the process whereby what was intimate becomes foreign. We experience that estrangement not vis-à-vis the new country: there, the process is the inverse: what was foreign becomes, little by little, familiar and beloved. The shocking, stupefying form of strangeness occurs not with an unknown woman we are trying to pick up but with a woman who used to belong to us. Only returning to the native land after a long absence can reveal the substantial strangeness of the world and of existence.

I think often of Gombrowicz in Berlin. Of his refusal

to see Poland again. Distrust toward the Communist regime still in power there? I don't think so: Polish Communism was already falling apart, cultivated people were almost all involved in the opposition, and they would have turned Gombrowicz's visit into a triumph. The real reasons for the refusal could only have been existential. And incommunicable. Incommunicable because too intimate. Incommunicable, also, because too wounding for the others. Some things we can only leave unsaid.

Stravinsky's Home

Stravinsky's life divides into three parts of roughly equal length: Russia: twenty-seven years; France and French Switzerland: twenty-nine years; America: thirty-two years.

The farewell to Russia was accomplished in several stages: Stravinsky is initially in France (starting in 1910) as if for a long study trip. These years are incidentally the most Russian in his creative work: *Petrushka, Zvezdoliki* (based on a work of the Russian poet Balmont), *Le Sacre du printemps, Pribaoutki,* the beginning of *Les Noces.* Then comes the war, and contacts with Russia become difficult; still, he remains a Russian composer with *Renard* and *Histoire du soldat,* inspired by the folk poetry of his homeland; only after the Revolution does he realize that his birthplace is lost to him, probably forever: the real emigration begins.

Emigration: a forced stay abroad for a person who considers his birthplace his only country. But the emigration stretches on and a new loyalty develops, this one to the adopted land; that's when the break occurs. Little by little, Stravinsky abandons Russian themes. He goes on in 1922 to write *Mavra* (a comic opera based on Pushkin); then, in 1928, *Le Baiser de la fée*, that recollection of Tchaikovsky; and thereafter, aside from some few marginal exceptions, he never returns to them. When he dies, in 1971, his wife, Vera, complying with his wishes, rejects the Soviet government's proposal to bury him in Russia and has him taken to the Venice cemetery.

Without a doubt, Stravinsky, like all the others, bore within him the wound of his emigration; without a doubt, his artistic evolution would have taken a different path if he had been able to stay where he was born. In fact, the start of his journey through the history of music coincides roughly with the moment when his native country ceases to exist for him; having understood that no country could replace it, he finds his only homeland in music; this is not just a nice lyrical conceit of mine, I think it in an absolutely concrete way: his only homeland, his only home, was music, all of music by all musicians, the very history of music; there he decided to establish himself, to take root, to live; there he ultimately found his only compatriots, his only intimates, his only neighbors, from Pérotin to Webern; it is with them that he began a long conversation, which ended only with his death.

He did all he could to feel at home there: he lingered in each room of that mansion, touched every corner, stroked every piece of the furniture; he went from the music of ancient folklore to Pergolesi, who gave him *Pulcinella* (1919), to the other Baroque masters, without whom his *Apollon Musagète* (1928) would be unimaginable, to Tchaikovsky, whose melodies he transcribes in *Le Baiser de la fée* (1928), to Bach, the godfather of his Concerto for Piano and Winds (1924) and Violin Concerto (1931) and whose Chorale Variations on *"Vom Himmel hoch"* he arranges (1956), to the jazz he celebrates in *Ragtime* for Eleven Instruments (1918), in *Piano-Rag Music* (1919), in *Preludium for Jazz Ensemble* (1937), and in *Ebony Concerto* (1945), to Pérotin and other old polyphonists, who inspire his *Symphony of Psalms* (1930) and especially his admirable *Mass* (1948), to Monteverdi, whom he studies in 1957, to Gesualdo, whose madrigals he transcribes in 1959, to Hugo Wolf, whose two songs he arranges (1968), and to the twelve-tone system, about which he initially was reserved but in which, eventually, after Schoenberg's death (1951), he recognized yet another room in his home.

His detractors, the defenders of music conceived as expression of feelings, who grew irate at his unbearably discreet "affective activity" and accused him of "poverty of heart," didn't have heart enough themselves to understand the wounded feelings that lay behind his vagabondage through the history of music.

But that's no surprise: no one is more insensitive than sentimental folk. Remember: "Heartlessness masked by a style overflowing with feeling."

PART FOUR

A Sentence

In "The Castrating Shadow of Saint Garta," I quoted one of those Kafka sentences that seem to concentrate all the originality of his novelistic poetry: the sentence in the third chapter of *The Castle* where Kafka describes the coition of K. and Frieda. To show precisely the specific beauty of Kafka's art, instead of using the existing French translations I decided to improvise my own most faithful possible translation. The differences between a Kafka sentence and its reflections in the mirror of translations have now brought me to the following remarks:

Translations

Let's review the translations.* The first is by Alexandre Vialatte, from 1938:

"Hours passed there, hours of mingled breaths, of

---

*Literal English versions of the three published French translations of Kafka's sentence are given here with the aim of enabling monolingual readers to understand the author's argument. These are followed by the German original with an exact English translation. For Vialatte, David, and Lortholary's translations, as well as the author's own translation into French, see the end of this part (pp. 116–117). (Translator.)

heartbeats in common, hours in which K. never ceased to experience the sensation that he was getting lost, that he had thrust in so far that no being before him had gone such a long way; abroad, in a country where even the air had none of the elements of his native air, where one must suffocate from exile and where all one could do, amid insane enticements, was to continue walking, continue getting lost."

It was recognized that Vialatte was a little too free with Kafka's text; that is why the publisher, Gallimard, decided to correct his translations for the 1976 publication of Kafka's novels in the Pléiade series. But Vialatte's heirs opposed this; and so an unprecedented solution was arrived at: Kafka's novels were published in Vialatte's faulty version, while the editor, Claude David, published his own corrections of the translation at the back of the book in the form of an amazing number of notes, such that, in order to reconstruct in his mind a "good" translation, the reader must constantly turn the pages to look at the notes. The combination of Vialatte's translation with the corrections in the back of the book actually constitutes a second French translation, which for simplicity's sake I'll simply refer to as "David":

"Hours passed there, hours of mingled breaths, of merged heartbeats, hours in which K. never ceased to experience the sensation that he was going astray, that he was thrusting farther than anyone ever had before him; he was in a foreign country, where even the very air no longer had anything in common with the air of his native country; the foreignness of this country choked him, and yet, among its mad enticements, one could only walk still farther, go still more astray."

Bernard Lortholary deserves great credit for having been radically dissatisfied with the existing translations and for retranslating Kafka's novels. His translation of *The Castle* dates from 1984:

"There hours passed, hours of mingled breathing, of hearts beating together, hours in which K. had the constant feeling of going astray, or of having advanced farther than any man into foreign lands, where the air itself had not a single element one could find in the air of one's native country, where one could only suffocate from the force of foreignness, yet without the power to do otherwise, in the midst of these absurd enticements, than to continue and go further astray."

Here now, the sentence in the original German:

"*Dort vergingen Stunden, Stunden gemeinsamen Atems, gemeinsamen Herzschlags, Stunden, in denen K. immerfort das Gefühl hatte, er verirre sich oder er sei so weit in der Fremde, wie vor ihm noch kein Mensch, einer Fremde, in der selbst die Luft keinen Bestandteil der Heimatluft habe, in der man vor Fremdheit ersticken müsse und in deren unsinnigen Verlockungen man doch nichts tun könne als weiter gehen, weiter sich verirren.*"

Of which this is an exact translation:

"There hours went by, hours of mutual breaths, of mutual heartbeats, hours in which K. continually had the feeling that he was going astray, or that he was farther inside the strange world than any person before him, in a strange world where the very air had in it no element of his native air, where one must suffocate from strangeness and where, in the midst of absurd enticements, one could do nothing but keep going, keep going astray."

Metaphor

The entire sentence is one long metaphor. Nothing requires more exactness from a translator than the translation of a metaphor. That is where we glimpse the core of an author's poetic originality. Vialatte's first error occurs with the verb *"s'enfoncer"* ("thrust" or "drive into"): *"il s'était enfoncé si loin"* ("he had thrust in so far"). In Kafka, K. doesn't thrust, he "is." The word *"s'enfoncer"* deforms the metaphor: it ties it too visually to real action (a man who makes love does thrust or drive) and thus deprives the metaphor of its *level of abstraction* (the *existential* nature of Kafka's metaphor does not seek to evoke—physically or visually—the act of love). David, in correcting Vialatte, keeps the same verb: *"s'enfoncer."* And even Lortholary (the most faithful) avoids the verb "to be," replacing it with *"s'avancer dans"* ("advance into").

In Kafka, while making love K. is *"in der Fremde"* ("in a strange place"); Kafka uses the word *"Fremde"* twice and then a third time in its derivative *"Fremdheit"* ("strangeness"): in the air of strange places, one suffocates from strangeness. All three translators are bothered by this threefold repetition: this is why Vialatte uses the word only once and instead of "strangeness" uses another word: "where one must suffocate from exile." But Kafka never mentions exile. Exile and strangeness are different notions. While making love, K. is not *driven away* from some home of his, not *banished* (and so not to be pitied); he is where he is by his own will, he is there because he has *dared* to be there. The word "exile" gives the metaphor an aura of martyrdom, of suffering—sentimentalizes and melodramatizes it.

The word *"Fremde"* is the only one in the sentence that cannot tolerate simple literal translation into French. Indeed, in German *"Fremde"* means not only "a foreign country" but also—more generally, more abstractly—everything that is strange, "a strange reality, a strange world." When *"in der Fremde"* is translated as *"à l'étranger,"* it is as if Kafka had used the term *"Ausland"* ("abroad"). The temptation to try for greater semantic exactness by translating the word *"Fremde"* into a two-word French term thus seems to me understandable; but in each of the actual solutions (Vialatte: *"à l'étranger, dans un* pays *où"* ["abroad, in a *country* where"]; David: *"dans un* pays *étranger"* ["in a foreign *country*"]; Lortholary: *"dans des* contrées *étrangères"* ["into foreign *regions*"]), the metaphor again loses the element of abstraction it has in Kafka, and its "touristic" quality is heightened rather than suppressed.

Metaphor as Phenomenological Definition

The idea that Kafka disliked metaphors should be corrected; he did dislike metaphors of a *certain kind*, but he is one of the great creators of the sort of metaphor I call *existential* or *phenomenological*. When Verlaine writes: "Hope glimmers like a wisp of straw in the cowshed," it is a superb *lyrical* flight of fancy. It is, however, unthinkable in Kafka's prose. For Kafka certainly disliked the lyricization of prose in novels.

Kafka's metaphorical imagination was no less rich than Verlaine's or Rilke's, but it was not lyrical: it was driven exclusively by the wish to decipher, to understand, to grasp the meaning of the characters' actions, the meaning of the situations in which they find themselves.

Let us recall another scene of coition, the one between Esch and Frau Hentjen in Broch's *The Sleepwalkers*: "His seeking mouth had found hers, which was now pressed against his like the muzzle of an animal against a pane of glass, and Esch was enraged because she kept her soul imprisoned behind her set teeth, to prevent him from possessing it."

The words "muzzle of an animal" and "pane of glass" are here not to evoke by comparison a visual image of the scene but to get at the *existential situation* of Esch, who even during the amorous embrace remains inexplicably separated (as by a pane of glass) from his mistress and unable to get hold of her soul (a prisoner behind set teeth). A situation difficult to catch—or, rather, uncatchable except by a metaphor.

At the beginning of Chapter Four of *The Castle* there is the second coition of K. and Frieda; it too is expressed in a single sentence (sentence-metaphor): "She was seeking something and he was seeking something, maddened, grimacing, heads thrusting into each other's chests as they sought, and their embraces and their tossing bodies did not make them forget but rather reminded them of the necessity to seek, as dogs desperately paw at the ground they pawed at each other's bodies, and, irremediably disappointed, to catch one last pleasure, each would from time to time sweep his tongue broadly across the other's face."

Just as the key words of the first coition's metaphor were "strange" and "strangeness," here the key words are "seek" and "paw at." These words do not express a visual image of what is happening but rather express an ineffable existential situation. When David, in his French translation, renders the passage above thus: "as dogs desperately *dig their claws* into the ground, they *dug their nails into each other's body*," he not only is being inaccurate (Kafka speaks neither of claws nor of nails that dig) but is also transferring the metaphor from the existential domain to the domain of visual description; by so doing, he places himself in a different aesthetic from Kafka's.

(This aesthetic discrepancy is still more evident in the last fragment of the sentence: Kafka says: "each would from time to time sweep his tongue broadly across the other's face"; in David, this precise and neutral observation turns into an expressionist metaphor: "each *whipped* the other's face with *blows* of the tongue.")

Richness of Vocabulary

Let's look at the verbs in the sentence: *vergehen* (went by—from the root *gehen*, go); *haben* (have); *sich verirren* (go astray); *sein* (be); *haben*; *ersticken müssen* (must suffocate); *tun können* (can do); *gehen*; *sich verirren*. Thus Kafka chooses the simplest, the most elementary verbs: go (twice), have (twice), go astray (twice), be, do, suffocate, must, can.

Translators tend to enrich the vocabulary: "never ceased to experience" (for "have"); "thrust," "advance," "go a long way" (for "be"); "find" (for "have").

(What terror the words "be" and "have" strike in all the translators in the world! They'll do anything to replace them with words they consider less routine.)

That tendency is understandable: what can the translator get credit for? For fidelity to the author's style? That's exactly what the readers in the translator's country have no way of judging. On the other hand, the public will automatically see richness of vocabulary as a value, as a performance, a proof of the translator's mastery and competence.

Now, richness of vocabulary is not a value in itself. The breadth of the vocabulary depends on the aesthetic intention governing the work. Carlos Fuentes' vocabulary is nearly dizzying in its richness. But Hemingway's is extremely narrow. The beauty of Fuentes' prose is bound up with richness, the beauty of Hemingway's with narrowness of vocabulary.

Kafka's vocabulary too is relatively restricted. That restriction has often been explained as one of Kafka's asceticisms. As his anti-aestheticism. As his indifference to beauty. Or as the cost exacted by Prague German, a language withering from being torn away from its popular roots. No one was willing to grant that this bareness of vocabulary expressed Kafka's *aesthetic intention*, that it was one of the distinctive marks of the *beauty* of his prose.

A General Remark on the Problem of Authority

For a translator, the supreme authority should be the *author's personal style*. But most translators obey another authority: that of the *conventional version* of "good French" (or good German, good English, etc.), namely, the French (the German, etc.) we learn in school. The translator considers himself the ambassador from that authority to the foreign author. That is the error: every author of some value *transgresses* against "good style," and in that transgression lies the originality (and hence the raison d'être) of his art. The translator's primary effort should be to understand that transgression. This is not difficult when it is obvious, as for example with Rabelais, or Joyce, or Céline. But there are authors whose transgression against "good style" is subtle, barely visible, hidden, discreet; as such, it is not easy to grasp. In such a case, it is all the more important to do so.

Repetition

Stunden (hours) occurs three times—repetition preserved in all three translations;

gemeinsamen (mutual) twice—repetition eliminated in all three translations;

sich verirren (go astray) twice—repetition preserved in all three translations;

die Fremde (strange) twice, and then once *die Fremdheit* (strangeness)—in Vialatte: "*à l'étranger*" (abroad) once, "strangeness" replaced by "exile"; in David and in Lortholary: once "foreign" (as an adjective) and once "foreignness";

die Luft (the air) twice—repetition preserved by all three translators;

haben (have) twice—the repetition exists in only one of the translations;

weiter (farther) twice—this repetition is replaced in Vialatte by repetition of the word "continue"; in David by the (weak) repetition of the word "still"; in Lortholary, the repetition has disappeared;

gehen, vergehen (go, went by)—this repetition (admittedly difficult to preserve) has disappeared in all three translations.

In general, we see that translators (obeying their schoolteachers) tend to limit repetitions.

The Semantic Meaning of Repetition

Twice *die Fremde*, once *die Fremdheit*: with this repetition the author introduced into his text a term with the quality of a key notion, a concept. If the author develops a lengthy line of thought from this word, repeating the word is necessary from the semantic and logical viewpoint. Suppose that, in order to avoid repetition, a Heidegger translator were to render "*das Sein*" once as "being," next as "existence," then as "life," then again as "human life," and finally as "being-there." Never knowing whether Heidegger is speaking of a single thing under different names or of different things, we would have not a scrupulously logical text but a mess. A novel's prose (I am speaking, of course, of novels worthy of the name) demands the same rigor (especially in meditative or metaphorical passages).

Another Remark on the Necessity of Preserving Repetitions

A bit farther on the same page of *The Castle*: "...*Stimme nach Frieda gerufen wurde. 'Frieda,' sagte K. in Friedas Ohr und gab so den Ruf weiter.*"

Literally, this means: "... a voice summoned Frieda. 'Frieda,' said K. in Frieda's ear, thus passing on the summons."

The French translators want to avoid the triple repetition of the name Frieda:

Vialatte: "'Frieda!' said he in *the maid's* ear, thus passing on . . . "

And David: "'Frieda,' said K. in *his companion's* ear, passing on to her . . . "

How false the words replacing Frieda's name sound! Note that in the text of *The Castle*, K. is never anything but K. In dialogue, others may call him "surveyor" or perhaps other things, but Kafka himself, the narrator, never refers to him by the words "stranger," "newcomer," "young man," or whatever. K. is nothing but K. And not only he but all the characters in Kafka always have just a single name, a single designation.

Thus Frieda is Frieda; not lover, not mistress, not companion, not maid, not waitress, not whore, not young woman, not girl, not friend, not girlfriend. Frieda.

The Melodic Importance of Repetition

There are moments when Kafka's prose takes flight
and becomes song. That is the case with the two sentences I have been considering. (Note that both of
these exceptionally beautiful sentences are descriptions
of the love act; this says a hundred times more than all
the biographers' research about the importance of
eroticism for Kafka. But let's go on.) Kafka's prose
takes flight on two wings: intensity of metaphorical
imagination and captivating melody.

Melodic beauty here is connected to the repetition
of words; the sentence begins: *"Dort vergingen*
Stunden, Stunden gemeinsamen *Atems*, gemeinsamen
Herzschlags, Stunden . . . "* ("There, *hours* went by,
hours of mutual breaths, *of mutual* heartbeats,
hours . . . ") In nine words, five repetitions. At the
middle of the sentence: the repetition of the word
"Fremde" ("strange") and the word *"Fremdheit"*
("strangeness"). And at the end of the sentence, yet
another repetition: ". . . weiter *gehen*, weiter *sich verirren*" (". . . *keep going, keep going* astray"). These multiple repetitions slow the tempo and give the sentence a
yearning cadence.

In the other sentence, K.'s second coition, we find
the same principle of repetition: the verb "seek"
repeated four times, the word "something" twice, the
word "body" twice, the verb "paw" twice; and let's not
forget the conjunction "and," which, against all the
rules of syntactic elegance, is repeated four times.

In German, that sentence begins: *"Sie suchte etwas
und er suchte etwas . . .* " Vialatte says something

entirely different: "She was seeking something and was seeking something again . . . " David corrects him: "She was seeking something and so was he, on his part." How odd: preferring to say "and so was he, on his part" rather than to translate literally Kafka's beautiful and simple repetition: "She was seeking something and he was seeking something . . . "

Repetition Skill

There's a skill to repetition. Because there certainly are bad, clumsy repetitions (as when, in the description of a dinner, the words "chair," "fork," and the like appear three times in two sentences). The rule: a word is repeated because it is important, because one wants its sound as well as its meaning to reverberate throughout a paragraph, a page.

Digression: An Example of the Beauty of Repetition

The very short (two-page) Hemingway story "One Reader Writes" is divided into three parts: 1) a brief paragraph describing a woman writing a letter "steadily with no necessity to cross out or rewrite anything"; 2) the letter itself, in which the woman speaks of her husband's venereal disease; 3) the interior monologue that follows it, quoted here:

"Maybe he can tell me what's right to do, she said to herself. Maybe he can tell me. In the picture in the paper he looks like he'd know. He looks smart, all right. Every day he tells somebody what to do. He ought to know. I want to do whatever is right. It's such a long time though. It's a long time. And it's been a long time. My Christ, it's been a long time. He had to go wherever they sent him, I know, but I don't know what he had to get it for. Oh, I wish to Christ he wouldn't have got it. I don't care what he did to get it. But I wish to Christ he hadn't ever got it. It does seem like he didn't have to have got it. I don't know what to do. I wish to Christ he hadn't got any kind of malady. I don't know why he had to get a malady."

The entrancing melody of this passage is based entirely on repetitions. They are not a device (like rhyme in poetry), but they come out of everyday spoken language, thoroughly unpolished language.

In addition: this very short story, it seems to me, is a unique instance in the history of prose fiction where the musical intention is primordial: without that melody the text would lose its raison d'être.

Breath

By his own account, Kafka wrote his long story "The Judgment" in a single night, without interruption, that is to say at extraordinary speed, letting himself be carried along by a practically uncontrolled imagination. Speed, which later became the surrealists' programmatic method ("automatic writing")—allowing for the liberation of the subconscious from supervision by reason, and making the imagination explode—played roughly the same role in Kafka.

Roused by that *methodical speed*, the Kafkan imagination runs like a river, a dreamlike river that finds no respite till a chapter's end. That long breath of imagination is reflected in the nature of the syntax: in Kafka's novels, there is a near absence of colons (except for those routinely introducing dialogue) and an exceptionally modest number of semicolons. The manuscripts (in the critical edition: Fischer, 1982) show that even commas seemingly required by the rules of syntax are often lacking. The texts are divided into very few paragraphs. This *tendency to minimize the articulation*—few paragraphs, few strong pauses (on rereading a manuscript, Kafka often even changed periods to commas), few markers emphasizing the text's logical organization (colons, semicolons)—is consubstantial with Kafka's style; at the same time it is a perpetual attack on "good German style" (as well as on the "good style" of all the languages into which Kafka is translated).

Kafka made no definitive version of *The Castle* for the printer, and one could reasonably assume that he might still have brought in this or that correction, including punctuation. So I am not enormously shocked (not pleased, either, obviously) that Max Brod, as Kafka's first editor, *from time to time* should have created a paragraph indentation or added a semicolon to make the text easier to read. Actually, even in Brod's edition, the *general character* of Kafka's syntax still shows clearly, and the novel preserves its great long breath.

Let's go back to that third-chapter sentence: it is relatively long, with commas but no semicolons (in the manuscript and in all the German editions). So what disturbs me most in the Vialatte version of this sentence is the added semicolon. It represents the end of a logical segment, a caesura that invites one to lower the voice, take a short pause. That caesura (although correct by the rules of syntax) chokes off Kafka's breath. David then even divides the sentence into three parts, with *two* semicolons. These two semicolons are all the more incongruous given that throughout the entire third chapter (according to the manuscript) Kafka uses only one semicolon. In the edition established by Max Brod there are thirteen. Vialatte reaches thirty-one. Lortholary twenty-eight, plus three colons.

Typographical Appearance

You can *see* the long, intoxicating flight of Kafka's prose in the text's typographical appearance, which is often a single "endless" paragraph, over pages, enfolding even long passages of dialogue. In Kafka's manuscript, the third chapter is divided into just two long paragraphs. In Brod's edition there are four. In Vialatte's translation, ninety. In Lortholary's translation, ninety-five. French editions of Kafka's novels have been subjected to an articulation that is not their own: paragraphs much more numerous, and therefore much shorter, which simulate a more logical, more rational organization of the text and which dramatize it, sharply separating all the dialogue exchanges.

In no translation into other languages, to my knowledge, has the original articulation of Kafka's texts been changed. Why have the French translators (all, unanimously) done this? They must certainly have had a reason for it. The Pléiade edition of Kafka's novels contains over five hundred pages of notes. Yet I find not a single sentence there giving such a reason.

And Finally, a Remark on Type, Large and Small

Kafka insisted that his books be printed in very large type. These days that is recalled with the indulgent smile prompted by great men's whims. Yet nothing about it warrants a smile; Kafka's wish was justified, logical, serious, related to his aesthetic, or, more specifically, to his way of articulating prose.

An author who divides his text into many short paragraphs will not insist so on large type: a lavishly articulated page can be read rather easily.

By contrast, a text that flows out in an endless paragraph is very much less legible. The eye finds no place to stop or rest, the lines are easily "lost track of." To be read with pleasure (that is, without eye fatigue), such a text requires relatively large type that makes reading easy and allows one to stop anytime to savor the beauty of the sentences.

I look through the German paperback edition of *The Castle*: on a small page, thirty-nine appallingly cramped lines of an "endless paragraph": it's illegible; or it's legible only as *information*; or as a *document*; in any case not as a text meant for aesthetic perception. In an appendix, on some forty pages: all the passages Kafka deleted from his manuscript. They disregard Kafka's desire (for thoroughly justified aesthetic reasons) to have his text printed in large type; they fish

out all the sentences he decided (for thoroughly justified aesthetic reasons) to destroy. In that indifference
to the author's aesthetic wishes is reflected all the sadness of the posthumous fate of Kafka's work.

FRENCH TRANSLATIONS OF THE SENTENCE

*Des heures passèrent là, des heures d'haleines mêlées, de
battements de coeur communs, des heures durant lesquelles
K. ne cessa d'éprouver l'impression qu'il se perdait, qu'il
s'était enfoncé si loin que nul être avant lui n'avait fait plus
de chemin; à l'étranger, dans un pays où l'air même n'avait
plus rien des éléments de l'air natal, où l'on devait étouffer
d'exil et où l'on ne pouvait plus rien faire, au milieu d'in-
sanes séductions, que continuer à marcher, que continuer à
se perdre.*

—Alexandre Vialatte

*Des heures passèrent là, des heures d'haleines mêlées, de
battements de coeur confondus, des heures durant lesquelles
K. ne cessa d'éprouver l'impression qu'il s'égarait, qu'il s'en-
fonçait plus loin qu'aucun être avant lui; il était dans un
pays étranger, où l'air même n'avait plus rien de commun
avec l'air du pays natal; l'étrangeté de ce pays faisait suffo-
quer et pourtant, parmi de folles séductions, on ne pouvait
que marcher toujours plus loin, s'égarer toujours plus avant.*

—Claude David

*Là passèrent des heures, des heures de respirations mêlées,
de coeurs battant ensemble, des heures durant lesquelles K.
avait le sentiment constant de s'égarer, ou bien de s'être
avancé plus loin que jamais aucun homme dans des contrées*

étrangères, où l'air lui-même n'avait pas un seul élément qu'on retrouvât dans l'air du pays natal, où l'on ne pouvait qu'étouffer à force d'étrangeté, sans pouvoir pourtant faire autre chose, au milieu de ces séductions insensées, que de continuer et de s'égarer davantage.

—Bernard Lortholary

Là, s'en allaient des heures, des heures d'haleines communes, de battements de coeur communs, des heures durant lesquelles K. avait sans cesse le sentiment qu'il s'égarait, ou bien qu'il était plus loin dans le monde étranger qu'aucun être avant lui, dans un monde étranger où l'air même n'avait aucun élément de l'air natal, où l'on devait étouffer d'étrangeté et où l'on ne pouvait rien faire, au milieu de séductions insensées, que continuer à aller, que continuer à s'égarer.

—Milan Kundera

PART FIVE

À la Recherche du Présent Perdu

1

In the middle of Spain, somewhere between Barcelona and Madrid, two people sit in the bar of a small railroad station: an American man and a girl. We know nothing about them except that they are waiting for the train to Madrid, where the girl is going to have an operation, certainly (though the word is never spoken) an abortion. We don't know who they are, how old they are, whether or not they are in love; we don't know the reasons that brought them to their decision. Their conversation, even though it is reproduced with extraordinary precision, gives us no understanding either of their motivations or of their past.

The girl is tense and the man is trying to calm her: "It's really an awfully simple operation, Jig. It's not really an operation at all." And then: "I'll go with you and I'll stay with you all the time. . . ." And then:

"We'll be fine afterward. Just like we were before."

When he senses the slightest agitation on the girl's part, he says: "Well, if you don't want to you don't have to. I wouldn't have you do it if you didn't want to." And eventually, again: "You've got to realize that I don't want you to do it if you don't want to. I'm perfectly willing to go through with it if it means anything to you."

Behind the girl's replies, one can sense her moral scruples. Looking at the landscape, she says: "And we could have all this. And we could have everything and every day we make it more impossible."

The man tries to calm her: "We can have everything. . . ."

"No. . . . And once they take it away, you never get it back."

And when the man again assures her that the operation is safe, she says: "Would you do something for me now?"

"I'd do anything for you."

"Would you please please please please please please please stop talking?"

The man says: "But I don't want you to. I don't care anything about it."

"I'll scream," says the girl.

At this point the tension reaches its peak. The man gets up to take their bags to the other side of the station, and when he returns: "Do you feel better?"

"I feel fine. There's nothing wrong with me. I feel fine." And these are the last lines of the famous story "Hills Like White Elephants," by Ernest Hemingway.

2

What is odd about this five-page story is that from the dialogue we can imagine any number of stories: the man is married and is forcing his mistress to have an abortion to spare his wife; he is a bachelor and wants the abortion because he is worried about complicating his life; but it is also possible that he is unselfishly looking ahead to the problems a child would cause the girl; maybe—anything is imaginable—he is seriously ill and is concerned about leaving the girl on her own with a child; we can even imagine that the child's father is some other man whom the girl left to go off with this one, who is advising her to have the abortion but stands ready, should she refuse, to take on the father role himself. And the girl? She might have agreed to the abortion to satisfy her lover; or maybe she took the initiative herself but, as the day approaches, is losing her nerve, feels guilty, and is engaging in some last verbal resistance, directed more at her own conscience than at her partner. Indeed, one could go on forever inventing the situations that might lie behind the dialogue.

As for the nature of the characters, the choice is just as great: the man could be sensitive, loving, tender; he could be selfish, wily, hypocritical. The girl could be hypersensitive, subtle, deeply moral; she could also be capricious, affected, fond of making hysterical scenes.

The real motives behind their behavior are the more unclear as the dialogue carries no indication of how the lines are spoken: fast? slow? ironically, ten-derly, mechanically, harshly, wearily? The man says: "You know I love you." The girl answers: "I know." But what does that "I know" mean? Does she really feel sure of the man's love? Or is she speaking ironically? And what does that irony mean? That the girl doesn't believe in his love? Or that this man's love no longer matters to her?

Apart from the dialogue, the story consists of only a few necessary descriptions; they are as scant as stage directions. Only one motif escapes this rule of maximum economy: the one of the white hills that stretch to the horizon; it returns several times, accompanied by a metaphor (more exactly: simile), the only one in the story. Hemingway was no lover of metaphors. Also, this one is not the narrator's, but the girl's; it is she who says, as she gazes at the hills: "They look like white elephants."

Swallowing his beer, the man answers: "I've never seen one."

"No, you wouldn't have."

"I might have," says the man. "Just because you say I wouldn't have doesn't prove anything."

In these four lines of dialogue, the characters reveal the difference, indeed the opposition, between them: the man shows some reserve toward the girl's poetic invention ("I've never seen one"), she snaps right back, seeming to reproach him for a lack of poetic sensitivity ("you wouldn't have"), and the man (as if already familiar with this reproach and allergic to it) defends himself ("I might have").

Later, when the man assures the girl of his love, she says: "But if I do it, then it will be nice again if I say things are like white elephants, and you'll like it?"

"I'll love it. I love it now but I just can't think about it."

So does this different attitude about metaphor at least distinguish between their characters? The girl subtle and poetic, the man literal-minded?

Well, all right, we could see the girl as more poetic than the man. But it's also possible to see her metaphor-find as mannerism, preciosity, affectation: wanting to be admired as original and imaginative, she shows off her little poetical flourishes. If that is the case, the ethical and emotional content of her remarks about the world that will no longer be theirs after the abortion can be attributed to her taste for lyrical exhibitionism rather than to the authentic despair of a woman giving up her motherhood.

No, there is nothing clear about whatever lies behind that simple and banal dialogue. Any man could say the same lines as this man, any woman the same as the girl. Whether a man loves a woman or not, whether he is lying or sincere, he would say the same thing. As though this dialogue were waiting here since the creation of the world to be delivered by countless couples, with no regard to their individual psychology.

Since they have nothing more to work out, it is impossible to make any moral judgment of these characters; as they sit in the train station, everything has already been definitively decided; they have already made their points a thousand times before; a thousand times already they have debated the arguments; now the old dispute (old discussion, old drama) shows only faintly through a conversation where nothing is at stake anymore, and words are just words.

3

Even though the story is extremely *abstract*, describing a quasi-archetypal situation, it is also extremely *concrete*, attempting to capture the visual and aural surface of a situation, of the dialogue in particular.

Try to reconstruct a dialogue from your own life, the dialogue of a quarrel or a dialogue of love. The most precious, the most important situations are utterly gone. Their abstract sense remains (I took this point of view, he took that one, I was aggressive, he was defensive), perhaps a detail or two, but the acousticovisual concreteness of the situation in all its continuity is lost.

And not only is it lost but we do not even wonder at this loss. We are resigned to losing the concreteness of the present. We immediately transform the present moment into its abstraction. We need only recount an episode we experienced a few hours ago: the dialogue contracts to a brief summary, the setting to a few general features. This applies to even the strongest memories, which affect the mind deeply, like a trauma: we are so dazzled by their potency that we don't realize how schematic and meager their content is.

When we study, discuss, analyze a reality, we analyze it as it appears in our mind, in our memory. We know reality only in the past tense. We do not know it as it is in the present, in the moment when it's happening, when it *is*. The present moment is unlike the memory of it. Remembering is not the negative of forgetting. Remembering is a form of forgetting.

We can assiduously keep a diary and note every event. Rereading the entries one day, we will see that they cannot evoke a single concrete image. And still worse: that the imagination is unable to help our memory along and reconstruct what has been forgotten. The present—the concreteness of the present—as a phenomenon to consider, as a *structure*, is for us an unknown planet; so we can neither hold on to it in our memory nor reconstruct it through imagination. We die without knowing what we have lived.

4

The need to resist the loss of the fleeting reality of the present arose for the novel, I think, only at a certain moment in its evolution. In Boccaccio the tale exemplifies the abstraction that the past becomes upon being recounted: without concrete scenes, nearly without dialogue, a kind of summary, it is a narration that gives us the essence of an event, the causal sequence of a story. The novelists who came after Boccaccio were fine storytellers, but capturing the concreteness of the present moment was neither their issue nor their goal. They were telling a story, without necessarily imagining it in concrete scenes.

The scene becomes the *basic* element of the novel's composition (the locus of the novelist's virtuosity) at the beginning of the nineteenth century. The novels of Scott, of Balzac, of Dostoyevsky, are composed as a series of minutely described scenes with their setting, their dialogue, their action; anything not connected with this series of scenes, anything that is not scene, is considered and felt to be secondary, even superfluous. The novel is like a very rich film script.

When the scene becomes the novel's basic element, the issue of reality as it occurs in the present is potentially raised. I say "potentially" because, in Balzac or in Dostoyevsky, what inspires the art of scene-making is more a passion for the dramatic than a passion for the concrete, more theater than reality. Actually, the novel's new aesthetic (the aesthetic born of this "second half" of the novel's history) shows in the *theatrical* nature of the construction: it is a construction that focuses a) on a single plot (as against "picaresque" construction, a series of different plots); b) on the same characters (letting characters leave the novel midway, which was normal in Cervantes, is now considered a flaw); c) on a narrow time span (even if much time elapses between the beginning and the end of the novel, the action itself unfolds over a few particular days; *The Possessed*, for example, stretches over several months, but all of its very complex action occurs on two, then three, then two, and finally five days).

In this Balzacian or Dostoyevskian construction, it is exclusively by means of the scenes that all the complexity of plot, all the richness of thought (the great dialogues of ideas in Dostoyevsky), all the psychology of the characters, must be expressed with clarity; that is why the scene, as it does in a play, becomes artificially concentrated, dense (multiple encounters in a single scene), and develops with an unnatural logical rigor (to bring out the conflict of interests and passions); in order to express everything that is essential (essential for the intelligibility of the action and its meaning), it must forgo everything that is "unessential," meaning everything banal, ordinary, quotidian, everything random, or mere atmosphere.

It was Flaubert ("our most respected, honored master," as Hemingway called him in a letter to Faulkner) who moved the novel away from theatricality. In his novels, the characters meet in an everyday setting, which (by its indifference, its indiscretion, but also by its moods and magic spells that make a situation beautiful and memorable) constantly intrudes on their intimacy. Emma is having a rendezvous with Léon in the church, but a guide latches onto them and interrupts their tête-à-tête with his long-winded, inane chatter. In his preface to *Madame Bovary*, Henry de Montherlant is ironic about the methodical nature of this way of bringing an antithetical motif into a scene, but the irony is misplaced; for it is not a matter of an *artistic mannerism*; it is a matter of a *discovery* that might be termed *ontological*: the discovery of the structure of the present moment; the discovery of the perpetual coexistence of the banal and the dramatic that underlies our lives.

Capturing the concreteness of the present has been one of the continuing trends that, since Flaubert, was to mark the evolution of the novel: it would reach its apogee, its very monument, in James Joyce's *Ulysses*, which in nearly eight hundred pages describes eighteen hours of life; Bloom stops in the street with McCoy: in a single second, between two successive lines of dialogue, endless numbers of things occur: Bloom's interior monologue; his gestures (hand in pocket, he touches the envelope of a love letter); everything he sees (a woman climbs into a carriage and allows a glimpse of her legs, etc.); everything he hears; everything he feels. In Joyce, a single second of the present becomes a little infinity.

5

In the epic and in the dramatic arts, the passion for the concrete has differing power; the evidence is in their dissimilar relation to prose. The epic abandoned verse around the sixteenth century, and so became a new art: the novel. Dramatic literature moved from verse to prose much later and much more slowly. Opera still later, at the turn of the twentieth century, with Charpentier (*Louise*, 1900), with Debussy (*Pelléas et Mélisande*, 1902, although it is written to very stylized, poetic prose), and with Janacek (*Jenufa*, composed between 1896 and 1903). The last is the creator of what I consider the most important opera aesthetic in the era of modern art. I say "I consider" because I don't wish to hide my personal passion for him. Yet I don't believe I am wrong, for Janacek's feat was tremendous: he discovered a new world for opera, the world of prose. I don't mean to say he was alone in doing so (the Berg of *Wozzeck*, 1925, which incidentally Janacek passionately championed, and even the Poulenc of *La Voix humaine*, 1959, do something close), but he pursued his goal in a particularly consistent way for thirty years, creating five major works that live on: *Jenufa*; *Katia Kabanova*, 1921; *The Cunning Little Vixen*, 1924; *The Makropulos Affair*, 1926; *From the House of the Dead*, 1928.

I've said he discovered the *world* of prose, for prose is not only a form of discourse distinct from verse; it is also an aspect of reality, its daily, concrete, momentary aspect, and the opposite of myth. This goes to the deepest conviction of every novelist: there is nothing so thoroughly disguised as the prose of life; every man seeks endlessly to transform his life into myth—seeks, so to speak, to transcribe it into verse, to shroud it in verse (bad verse). If the novel is an art and not merely a "literary genre," the reason is that the discovery of prose is its *ontological mission*, which no art but the novel can take on entirely.

On the novel's path toward the mystery of prose, into the beauty of prose (for, being an art, the novel discovers prose as beauty), Flaubert made an enormous stride. In the history of opera, a half century later, Janacek accomplished that same Flaubertian revolution. But whereas we find this completely natural in a novel (as if the scene between Emma and Rodolphe against the agricultural-fair background were encoded in the genes of the novel form as an almost inevitable possibility), in opera it is far more shocking, audacious, unexpected: it contravenes the principle of unrealism and extreme stylization that seemed inseparable from the very essence of opera.

To the extent that they ventured into opera, the great modernists most often took the path of an even more radical stylization than had their nineteenth-century predecessors: Honegger turned to legendary or biblical subjects, and then gave them a form that oscillates between opera and oratorio; the subject of Bartók's only opera is a symbolist fable; Schoenberg wrote two operas: one is an allegory, the other dramatizes an extreme situation at the edge of madness. Stravinsky's operas are all written on verse texts and are extremely stylized. Janacek thus went not only against the tradition of opera but also against the prevailing trend of modern opera.

6

A famous drawing: a short, mustached man with thick white hair is walking along with an open notebook in his hand, writing down in music notes the talk he hears on the street. It was his passion: to put the living word into musical notation; he left a hundred of these "intonations of spoken language." In the eyes of his contemporaries, this odd activity put him at best among the eccentrics and at worst among the naïve who did not understand that music is a created thing and not the naturalistic imitation of life.

But the question is not: should one imitate life or not? The question is: should a musician acknowledge the existence of the world of sound outside of music, and study it? His studies of spoken language can throw light on two basic aspects of Janacek's music:

1) *his melodic originality*: toward the end of the Romantic movement, the melodic wealth of European music seemed to be running out (there is indeed an arithmetical limit to the permutations of seven or twelve tones); close knowledge of the intonations that come not from music but from the objective world of words allowed Janacek access to a different inspiration, a different source of melodic imagination; in consequence, his melodies (he may be the last great melodist in the history of music) have a very specific character and are immediately recognizable:

a) contrary to Stravinsky's maxim ("Be frugal with your intervals, treat them like dollars"), they contain many unusually large intervals, till then unthinkable in a "beautiful" melody;

b) they are very succinct, compressed, and nearly

impossible to develop, prolong, elaborate by techniques common till then, which would immediately make them false, artificial, "deceitful"; that is: his melodies are developed in their own particular way: either repeated (persistently repeated) or else treated like a word: for example, progressively *intensified* (on the model of someone insisting or imploring), etc.;

2) *his psychological orientation*: what most interested Janacek in his research on spoken language was not the specific rhythm of the language (the Czech language) or its prosody (there is no recitative in Janacek's operas), but the influence on spoken intonation of a speaker's shifting psychological state; he sought to comprehend the *semantics of melodies* (he thus appears to be the antipode of Stravinsky, who conceded music no expressive capacity; for Janacek, only the note that is expression, that is emotion, has the right to exist); examining the connection between an intonation and an emotion, Janacek the musician acquired a thoroughly unique psychological lucidity; a veritable *psychological furor* (remember Adorno speaking of Stravinsky's "antipsychological furor") marked all of his work; because of it he turned especially to opera, for in opera the ability to "define emotions musically" could be realized and tested better than anywhere else.

7

What is a conversation in real life, in the concreteness of the present moment? We don't know. All we know is that conversations on the stage, in a novel, or even on the radio are not like a real conversation. This was certainly one of Hemingway's artistic obsessions: to catch the structure of real conversation. Let us try to define this structure by comparing it with that of theatrical dialogue:

a) *in the theater*: the story is told in and through the dialogue; this is therefore focused entirely on the action, on its meaning, on its content; *in real life*: dialogue is surrounded by dailiness, which interrupts it, slows it down, affects its development, changes its course, makes it unsystematic and illogical;

b) *in the theater*: dialogue must provide the audience with the most intelligible, the clearest, idea of the dramatic conflict and of the characters; *in real life*: the individuals conversing know each other and know the subject of their conversation; thus their dialogue is never wholly comprehensible to a third person; it remains enigmatic, a thin veneer of the said over the immensity of the unsaid;

c) *in the theater*: the limited time span of the performance demands a maximal economy of words in the dialogue; *in real life*: the characters return to a subject already discussed, repeat themselves, correct what they just said, etc.; these repetitions and awkwardnesses reveal the characters' obsessions and imbue the conversation with a particular melody.

Hemingway knew not only how to catch the structure of real dialogue but also how to use it to create a *form*—a simple, transparent, limpid, beautiful form, as appears in "Hills Like White Elephants": the conversation between the American man and the girl begins *piano*, with insignificant remarks; the repetitions of the same words, the same turns of phrase, throughout the story give it a melodic unity (this melodization of dialogue is what is so striking in Hemingway, so entrancing); the intervention of the woman bringing drinks curbs the tension, which nonetheless goes on rising, reaches its crisis toward the end ("please please"), then calms to *pianissimo* with the final words.

8

"February 15 toward evening. Twilight at 6, near the railroad station. Two young women are waiting for someone.

"On the sidewalk, the bigger one, her cheeks rosy, in a red winter coat, shivers.

"She starts speaking brusquely:

"'We're going to wait here and I know he won't show up.'

"Her companion, cheeks pale, in a flimsy skirt, interrupts the last note with a somber, sad, soulful echo:

"'I don't care.'

"And she stayed put, half rebellious, half waiting."

So begins one of the texts Janacek regularly published, together with his musical notations, in a Czech periodical.

Imagine that the sentence "We're going to wait here and I know he won't show up" is a line in a story an actor is reading aloud to an audience. We would probably sense a certain falseness in his tone. He speaks the sentence as one might imagine it in memory; or, simply, in a way meant to move his listeners. But how is this sentence spoken in a real situation? What is the *melodic truth* of this sentence? What is the melodic truth of a vanished moment?

The search for the vanished present; the search for the melodic truth of a moment; the wish to surprise and capture this fleeting truth; the wish to plumb by that means the mystery of the immediate reality constantly deserting our lives, which thereby becomes the thing we know least about. This, I think, is the ontological import of Janacek's studies of spoken language and, perhaps, the ontological import of all his music.

Act Two of *Jenufa*: after lying ill for some days with puerperal fever, Jenufa leaves her bed and learns that her newborn son is dead. Her reaction is unexpected: "So, he is dead. So, he has become a little angel." And she sings these phrases calmly, with a strange astonishment, as if paralyzed, without cries, without gestures. The melodic curve rises several times, only to fall back immediately, as if it too were stricken with paralysis; it is beautiful, it is moving, yet without losing its *accuracy*.

Novak, the most influential Czech composer of the time, ridiculed this scene: "It's as if Jenufa were mourning the death of her parrot." It's all there, in this idiotic sarcasm. To be sure, this is not how we imagine a woman who is just learning of her child's death! But an event as we imagine it hasn't much to do with the same event as it *is* when it happens.

Janacek based his first operas on "realist" plays; in his time, doing that in itself shattered conventions; but because of his thirst for the concrete, even the prose drama form soon came to seem artificial to him: and so he wrote his own libretti for his two most audacious operas, the one, for *The Cunning Little Vixen*, based on a newspaper serial, the other on Dostoyevsky—not on one of the writer's novels (ensnarement by the unnatural and the theatrical is a greater threat in Dostoyevsky's novels than anywhere else!), but on his "reportage" of the Siberian prison camp: *From the House of the Dead.*

Like Flaubert, Janacek was fascinated by the coexistence of various emotional charges in a single scene (he felt the Flaubertian fascination for "antithetical motifs"); thus his orchestra does not emphasize but instead often contradicts the emotional content of the words. There is one scene of *The Cunning Little Vixen* that I have always found particularly moving: in a forest inn, a gamekeeper, a village schoolmaster, and the innkeeper's wife are gossiping: they recall their absent friends and talk about the innkeeper, who is away that day in town, about the parish priest, who has moved house, about the woman the schoolmaster loved, who has just married someone else. The conversation is completely banal (never before Janacek had a situation so undramatic and so ordinary been seen on the opera stage), but the orchestra is full of a nearly unbearable yearning, so that the scene becomes one of the most beautiful elegies ever written on the transience of time.

9

For fourteen years, a certain Kovarovic, a conductor and submediocre composer who was director of the Prague Opera, rejected *Jenufa*. Although he finally gave in (in 1916 it was he who conducted the Prague premiere), he nonetheless held to his view of Janacek as a dilettante and made many changes in the score, revisions of the orchestration, and even a great number of deletions.

Didn't Janacek rebel? Certainly, but as we know, everything depends on the balance of power. And he was the weaker one. He was sixty-two years old and nearly unknown. If he fought too much, he could have had to wait another ten years for the premiere of his opera. Besides, even his supporters, euphoric over their master's unexpected success, all agreed: Kovarovic had done a magnificent job! For example, the final scene!

The final scene: After the body of Jenufa's illegitimate child is discovered drowned, after the stepmother has confessed her crime and the police have taken her away, Jenufa and Laca are left alone. Laca, the man over whom Jenufa preferred another but who loves her still, decides to stay with her. All that lies before this couple are misery, shame, and exile. An extraordinary mood: resigned, sorrowful, and yet glowing with immense compassion. Harp and strings, the soft sonority of the orchestra; the great drama closes, unexpectedly, with tranquil song, touching and intimate.

But can an opera end like that? Kovarovic transformed it into a real apotheosis of love. Who would dare object to an apotheosis? Besides, an apotheosis is so simple: you add brasses to extend the melody by contrapuntal imitation. An effective procedure, tried and proven a thousand times over. Kovarovic knew his business.

Snubbed and humiliated by his Czech compatriots, Janacek found firm and faithful support from Max Brod. But when Brod studied the score of *The Cunning Little Vixen*, he was not satisfied with the ending. The last words of the opera: a joke by a little frog stammering to the gamekeeper: "What y-y-you think you're seeing is n-n-not me, it's m-m-my grandpa." "Ending with the frog is impossible," Brod protested in a letter (*"Mit dem Frosch zu schliessen, ist unmöglich"*), and he proposed as a new last line a solemn proclamation to be sung by the gamekeeper: about nature's renewal, about the eternal power of youth. Another apotheosis.

But this time Janacek didn't obey. Now recognized outside his own country, he was no longer weak. By the time of the premiere of *From the House of the Dead*, he had become so again; he was dead. The ending of the opera is masterly: the hero is released from the camp. "Freedom! Freedom!" the convicts cry. Then the commandant shouts: "Back to work!" and these are the last words of the opera, which closes with the brutal rhythm of forced labor punctuated by the syncopated rattle of chains. The posthumous premiere was conducted by a pupil of Janacek's (who also prepared the barely finished manuscript of the score for publication). He fiddled a bit with the final pages: thus the cry "Freedom! Freedom!" returns at the end, and broadened into a tacked-on long coda, a joyous coda, an apotheosis (still another one). It is not an addition that, by repetition, extends the author's intent; it is the denial of that intent; the final lie that annuls the truth of the opera.

10

I open the biography of Hemingway published in 1985 by Jeffrey Meyers, a professor of literature in an American university, and I read the passage on "Hills Like White Elephants." The first thing I learn: the story "may . . . portray Hemingway's response to Hadley's [his first wife's] second pregnancy." There follows this commentary, which I accompany with my own italicized remarks in brackets:

"The comparison of hills with white elephants—imaginary animals that represent useless items, like the unwanted baby—is crucial to the meaning [*the comparison, a bit forced, of elephants with unwanted babies is not Hemingway's but the professor's; it is needed to set up the sentimental interpretation of the story*]. The simile becomes a focus of contention and establishes an opposition between the imaginative woman, who is moved by the landscape, and the literal-minded man, who refuses to sympathize with her point of view. . . . The theme of the story evolves from a series of polarities: natural v. unnatural, instinctive v. rational, reflective v. talkative, vital v. morbid [*the professor's intention becomes clear: to make the woman the morally positive pole, the man the morally negative pole*]. The egoistic man [*there is no reason to call the man egoistic*, unaware of the woman's feelings [*there is no reason to say this*], tries to bully her into having an abortion . . . so they can be exactly as they were before. . . . The woman, who finds it horribly unnatural, is frightened of killing the baby [*she cannot kill the baby, given that it is unborn*] and hurting herself. Everything the man says is false [*no: everything the man says is ordinary words of consolation, the only kind possible in such a situation*]; everything the woman says is ironic [*there are many other explanations for the girl's remarks*]. He forces her to consent to this operation [*"I wouldn't have you do it if you didn't want to," he says twice, and there is nothing to show that he is insincere*] in order to regain his love [*there is nothing to show either that she had the man's love or that she had lost it*], but the very fact that he can ask her to do such a thing means that she can never love him again [*there is no way to know what will happen after the scene in the railroad station*]. She agrees to this form of self-destruction [*the destruction of a fetus and the destruction of a woman are not the same thing*] after reaching the kind of dissociation of self that was portrayed in Dostoyevsky's Underground Man and in Kafka's Joseph K., and that reflects his attitude toward her: 'Then I'll do it. Because I don't care about me.' [*Reflecting someone else's attitude is not a dissociation, otherwise all children who obey their parents would be dissociated and would be like Josef K.*] She then walks away from him and . . . finds comfort in nature: in the fields of grain, the trees, the river and the hills beyond. Her peaceful contemplation [*we know nothing about the feelings that the sight of nature stirs in the girl; but in any case they are not peaceful feelings, for the words she speaks immediately afterward are bitter*] recalls Psalm 121 as she lifts up her eyes to the hills for help [*the plainer Hemingway's style, the more pretentious his commentator's*]. But her mood is shattered by the man's persistent argument [*let's read the story carefully: it is not the American man, it is the girl who, after her brief withdrawal, is the first to speak and continues the argument; the man is not looking for an argument, he only wants to calm the girl down*], which drives her to the edge of a breakdown. Echoing King Lear's 'Never, never, never, never, never,' she frantically begs: 'Would you please, please, please, please, please, please, please stop talking?' [*the evocation of Shakespeare is as meaningless as were those of Dostoyevsky and Kafka*]."

Let us summarize the summary:

1) In the American professor's interpretation, the short story is transformed into a moral lesson: the characters are judged according to their attitude toward abortion, which is a priori considered an evil: thus the woman ("imaginative," "moved by the landscape") represents the natural, the living, the instinctive, the reflective; the man ("egoistic," "literal-minded") represents the artificial, the rational, the chatty, the unhealthy (note incidentally that in modern moral discourse, the rational represents evil and the instinctive represents good);

2) the connection to the author's biography suggests that the negative, immoral hero is Hemingway himself, who is making a kind of confession through the intermediary of the story; in that case the dialogue loses all its enigmatic quality, the characters are without mystery and, for anyone who has read Hemingway's biography, thoroughly determined and clear;

3) the original aesthetic nature of the story (its lack of psychologizing, its intentional veiling of the characters' pasts, its undramatic nature, etc.) is not considered; worse, that aesthetic nature is *undone*;

4) starting with the basic givens of the story (a

man and a girl are on their way to an abortion), the professor goes on to invent his own story: an *egoistic* man is engaged in forcing *his wife* to have an abortion; the wife *despises* her husband, whom *she will never again be able to love*;

5) this other story is absolutely flat and all clichés; nevertheless, because it is compared successively with Dostoyevsky, Kafka, the Bible, and Shakespeare (the professor has managed to assemble in one paragraph the greatest authorities of all time), it retains its status as a great work and therefore, despite its author's moral poverty, justifies the professor's interest in it.

11

This is how kitsch-making interpretation kills off works of art. Some forty years before the American professor imposed this moralizing meaning on the story, "Hills Like White Elephants" was published in France under the title *"Paradis perdu,"* a title that has no relation to Hemingway (in no other language does the story bear this title) and that suggests the same meaning (paradise lost: preabortion innocence, happiness of impending motherhood, etc., etc.).

Kitsch-making interpretation is actually not the personal defect of some American professor or some early-twentieth-century Prague conductor (many conductors after him have ratified his alterations of *Jenufa*); it is a seduction that comes out of the collective unconscious; a command from the metaphysical prompter; a perennial social imperative; a force. That force is aimed not at art alone but primarily at reality itself. It does the opposite of what Flaubert, Janacek, Joyce, and Hemingway did. It throws a veil of commonplaces over the present moment, in order that the face of the real will disappear.

So that you shall never know what you have lived.

PART SIX

Works and Spiders

1

"I think." Nietzsche cast doubt on this assertion dictated by a grammatical convention that every verb must have a subject. Actually, said he, "a thought comes when 'it' wants to, and not when 'I' want it to; so that it is falsifying the fact to say that the subject 'I' is necessary to the verb 'think.'" A thought comes to the philosopher "from outside, from above or below, like events or thunderbolts heading for him." It comes in a rush. For Nietzsche loves "a bold and exuberant intellectuality that runs *presto*," and he makes fun of the savants for whom thought seems "a slow, halting activity, something like drudgery, often enough worth the sweat of the hero-savants, but nothing like that light, divine thing that is such close kin to dance and to high-spirited gaiety."

Elsewhere Nietzsche writes that the philosopher "must not, through some false arrangement of deduction and dialectic, falsify the things and the ideas he arrived at by another route. . . . We should neither conceal nor corrupt the actual way our thoughts come to us. The most profound and inexhaustible books will surely always have something of the aphoristic, abrupt quality of Pascal's *Pensées*."

We should not "corrupt the actual way our thoughts come to us": I find this injunction remarkable; and I notice that, beginning with *The Dawn*, all the chapters in all his books are written *in a single paragraph*: this is so that a thought should be uttered in one single breath; so that it should be caught the way it appeared as it sped toward the philosopher, swift and dancing.

2

Nietzsche's determination to preserve "the actual way" his thoughts come to him is inseparable from another of his injunctions, which charms me as much as the first: to resist the temptation to turn one's ideas into a system. Philosophical systems "these days stand in a distressed and discouraged posture. If they are indeed still standing." The attack is aimed at the inevitable dogmatism of systematizing thought as much as at its form: "an act put on by the systems-makers: in their desire to *fill in their system* and round off the horizon that encloses it, they must try to present *their weak points in the same style as their strong points*."

The italics above are mine: a philosophical treatise that expounds a system is doomed to include some weak passages; not because the philosopher is untalented but because the treatise form requires it; for before he gets to his innovative ideas, the philosopher

must explain what others say about the problem, must
refute them, propose other solutions, choose the best of
them and adduce arguments for it—a surprising argument alongside an obvious one, etc.—and the reader
yearns to skip pages and cut to the heart of the matter,
to the philosopher's new idea. In his *Aesthetics*, Hegel
gives us an image of art that is a superb synthesis; we
are fascinated by this eagle's-eye overview; but the text
itself is far from fascinating, it does not make us see
the thought as alluring as it looked when it was speeding toward the philosopher. In his desire to fill in his
system, Hegel describes every detail, square by square,
inch by inch, so that his *Aesthetics* comes across as a
collaboration between an eagle and hundreds of heroic
spiders spinning webs to cover all the crannies.

3

For André Breton (in his *Manifesto of Surrealism*), the
novel is an "inferior genre"; its style is one of "information pure and simple"; the nature of the information given is "needlessly specific" ("I am spared not a
single one of the hesitations over a character: shall he
be blond? what should he be called?. . . "); and the
descriptions: "there is nothing like the vacuity of these
passages; they are just piles of stock images"; as an
example there follows a paragraph quoted from *Crime
and Punishment*, a description of Raskolnikov's room,
with this comment: "Some will argue that this academic drawing is appropriate here, that at this point in
the novel the author has his reasons for loading me
down." But Breton considers these reasons unpersua-

sive, because: "I don't register the null moments in my life." Then, psychology: the lengthy expositions that tell us everything in advance: "this hero, whose actions and reactions are admirably anticipated, must not foil—though seeming likely to foil—the calculations of which he is the object."

However partisan this critique, we cannot ignore it; it does accurately express modern art's reservations toward the novel. To recapitulate: data; description; pointless attention to the null moments of existence; a psychology that makes the characters' every move predictable; in short, to roll all the complaints into one, it is the fatal lack of poetry that makes the novel an inferior genre for Breton. I am speaking of poetry as vaunted by the surrealists and the whole of modern art—poetry not as a literary genre, versified writing, but as a certain concept of beauty, as an explosion of the marvelous, a sublime moment of life, concentrated emotion, freshness of vision, fascinating surprise. For Breton, the novel is *nonpoetry* par excellence.

4

The fugue: a single theme sets off a chain of melodies in counterpoint, a stream that over its long course keeps the same character, the same rhythmic pulse, a single entity. After Bach, in music's Classical period, everything changes: the melodic theme becomes self-contained and short; its brevity makes monothematic composition nearly impossible; in order to construct a *large-scale work* (by this I mean: the architectural organization of a big-volume ensemble), the composer must follow one theme with another; thus is born a new art of composition which, as an example, grows into the sonata, the ruling form of the Classical and Romantic eras.

Following one theme with another called for intermediate passages, or *bridges*, as César Franck called them. The word "bridge" makes explicit that in a composition some passages are significant in themselves (the themes) and other passages are there to serve the former and haven't the same intensity or importance. Hearing Beethoven, one has the sense that the level of intensity changes constantly: at various times something is coming, then it arrives, then it's gone and something else is on its way.

An intrinsic contradiction in the music of the "second half" (the Classical and the Romantic): it considers its raison d'être the capacity to express emotions, but at the same time it elaborates its bridges, its codas, its development sections, which are demanded by the form alone, the residue of a proficiency that is completely impersonal, that is learned, and that has difficulty refraining from routine or from commonplace musical formulas (which occur sometimes in even the greatest, Mozart or Beethoven, but which abound in their lesser contemporaries). Thus inspiration and technique are always in danger of disconnecting; a *dichotomy* arises between the spontaneous and the worked-over; between material that seeks to express emotion directly and a technical development of that emotion as set into music; between the themes and the *filler* (a pejorative term but a thoroughly objective one: for it really is necessary to "fill out," horizontally, the time between themes and, vertically, the orchestral sound).

There is a story about Mussorgsky playing a Schumann symphony on the piano and stopping just before the development section to shout: "Here's where the musical mathematics starts!" It is this aspect—contrived, pedantic, intellectual, academic, uninspired—that made Debussy say that after Beethoven, symphonies became "studied, rigid exercises" and that the music of Brahms and Tchaikovsky "are competing for the boredom monopoly."

5

That intrinsic dichotomy does not make Classical or Romantic music inferior to the music of other eras; every era's art has its structural problems; that is what lures the artist to search for original solutions and thereby sets off the evolution of form. And the music of the second half was aware of this problem. Beethoven: he breathed an unprecedented expressive intensity into music, and at the same time, more than anyone else, he crafted the compositional technique of the sonata: that dichotomy must therefore have weighed especially heavily on him; to overcome it (not that he always succeeded), he devised various strategies:

—for instance, endowing musical material other than the themes—a scale, an arpeggio, a transition, a coda—with a startling expressiveness;

—or (for instance) giving another dimension to variation form, which, before him, was usually mere technical virtuosity, and rather frivolous virtuosity at that: like having a single fashion model strut the runway in different outfits. Beethoven elevates this form into a great musical meditation: what melodic, rhythmic, harmonic possibilities lie concealed within a theme? How far can one go in transforming a theme without betraying its essence? And what, in fact, is its esssence? In composing his variations, Beethoven needs none of the elements the sonata form calls for—neither bridges nor development sections nor any filler; never for a moment did he move outside what he believes essential, outside the mystery of the theme.

It would be interesting to examine all the music of the nineteenth century as a constant effort to overcome its structural dichotomy. In this connection, what I call *Chopin's strategy* comes to mind. Just as Chekhov never wrote a novel, so Chopin disdained *large-scale composition* and almost exclusively wrote collections of short pieces (mazurkas, polonaises, nocturnes, etc.). (Some exceptions prove the rule: his piano concertos are weak.) This was operating against the spirit of his time, which considered the creation of a symphony, a concerto, a quartet, the compulsory criterion of a composer's significance. But precisely in sidestepping this criterion, Chopin created a body of work that, perhaps alone of its time, has aged not at all and will remain *fully* alive, almost without exception. For me, *Chopin's strategy* explains why in Schumann, Schubert, Dvorak, Brahms the pieces of lesser size, lesser sonority, seem more alive, more beautiful (often *very* beautiful), than the symphonies and concertos. For (an important observation) the intrinsic dichotomy in the music of the second half is a problem only for *large-scale composition*.

6

In criticizing the art of the novel, is Breton attacking its weaknesses or its very essence? Let us note, first of all, that he is attacking the aesthetic of the novel that came into being early in the nineteenth century, with Balzac. The novel was in fullest flush then, for the first time establishing itself as an immense social force; armed with a nearly hypnotic power of seduction, it prefigured cinema art: so lifelike are its scenes on the screen of his imagination that a reader is prone to confuse them with scenes from his own life; to enthrall his reader, the novelist has available a whole *apparatus for fabricating the illusion of reality*; yet this apparatus generates for the novel a structural dichotomy like the one in Classical and Romantic music:

since it is meticulous causal logic that makes events convincing, no link of the chain can be omitted (however devoid of interest it may be in itself);

since the characters must appear to be "living," as much data about them as possible must be reported (however unremarkable);

and then there is history: its slow pace used to make it almost invisible, then it picked up speed and suddenly (here is Balzac's great experience), in the course of people's lifetimes, *everything* around them is changing—the streets they walk on, the furniture in their houses, the institutions they live by; *the background* of human lives is no longer an immobile, predictable stage set; it turns changeable, today's look doomed to be gone tomorrow, and so it is important to seize it, to paint it (no matter how tiresome these pictures of time passing might be).

Background: painting discovered it during the Renaissance, along with perspective, which divided the picture between what is up front and what is in the rear. This produced painting's particular formal problem; the portrait, for example: the face commands more attention and interest than the body does, and still more than the drapery behind. This is quite normal, this is how we see the world around us, but nonetheless, what is normal in life does not correspond to the formal requirements of art: the imbalance, in a painting, between the privileged areas and those that are, a priori, secondary still had to be compensated for, remedied, brought back into balance. Or else radically set aside, through a new aesthetic that would cancel out that dichotomy.

7

After 1948, through the years of Communist revolution in my native country, I saw the eminent role played by lyrical blindness in a time of Terror, which for me was the period when "the poet reigned along with the hangman." (*Life Is Elsewhere*). I would think about Mayakovsky then; his genius was as indispensable to the Russian Revolution as Dzherzhinsky's police. Lyricism, lyricization, lyrical talk, lyrical enthusiasm are an integrating part of what is called the totalitarian world; that world is not the gulag as such; it's a gulag that has poems plastering its outside walls and people dancing before them.

More than the Terror, the lyricization of the Terror was a trauma for me. It immunized me for good against all lyrical temptations. The only thing I deeply, avidly, wanted was a lucid, unillusioned eye. I finally found it in the art of the novel. This is why for me being a novelist was more than just working in one "literary genre" rather than another; it was an outlook, a wisdom, a position; a position that would rule out identification with any politics, any religion, any ideology, any moral doctrine, any group; a considered, stubborn, furious *nonidentification*, conceived not as evasion or passivity but as resistance, defiance, rebellion. I wound up having some odd conversations: "Are you a Communist, Mr. Kundera?" "No, I'm a novelist." "Are you a dissident?" "No, I'm a novelist." "Are you on the left or the right?" "Neither. I'm a novelist."

Since early youth, I have been in love with modern art—with its painting, its music, its poetry. But modern art was marked by its "lyrical spirit," by its illusions of progress, its ideology of the double revolution, aesthetic and political, and little by little, I took a dislike to all that. Yet my skepticism about the *spirit* of the avant-garde never managed to affect in the slightest my love for the *works* of modern art. I loved them, and I loved them all the more for being the first victims of Stalinist persecution; in *The Joke*, Cenek is sent to a disciplinary regiment because he loves cubist painting; that's how it was then: the Revolution had decided that modern art was its ideological Enemy Number One even though the poor modernists wanted only to sing its praises; I'll never forget Konstantin Biebl: an exquisite poet (ah, how many of his lines I knew by heart!) who, as an enthusiastic Communist, after 1948 took to writing propaganda poetry of a mediocrity as alarming as it was heartbreaking; shortly thereafter, he threw himself from a window onto a Prague pavement and died; in this subtle being, I saw modern art betrayed, cuckolded, martyred, assassinated, self-destroyed.

My allegiance to modern art was thus as much a passion as my love for the antilyricism of the novel. The poetic values dear to Breton, dear to all modern art (intensity, density, the unbound imagination, scorn for "the null moments of life"), I went seeking only in the unillusioned territory of the novel. But that made them all the more important to me. Which may explain why I was particularly allergic to the kind of boredom that irritated Debussy when he listened to the symphonies of Brahms or Tchaikovsky; allergic to the rustle of spiders hard at work. Which may explain why I long remained deaf to Balzac's art and why the novelist I particularly adored was Rabelais.

8

The dichotomy between themes and bridges, between foreground and background, is unknown to Rabelais. He moves nimbly from a grave topic to a list of the methods the little Gargantua invented for wiping his ass, and yet, aesthetically, all these elements, frivolous or grave, have equal importance in his work, give me equal pleasure. That is what delighted me about him and about other early novelists: they talk about what fascinates them and they stop when the fascination stops. Their freedom of composition set me dreaming: of writing without fabricating suspense, without constructing a plot and working up its plausibility, of writing without describing a period, a milieu, a city; of abandoning all that and holding on to only the essential; that is to say: creating a work in which the bridges and the filler have no reason to be and in which the novelist would never be forced—for the sake of form and its dictates—to stray by even a single line from what he cares about, what fascinates him.

9

Modern art: a revolt against the imitation of reality, in the name of the autonomous laws of art. One of the first practical requirements of this autonomy: that all the moments, all the particles of a work have equal aesthetic importance.

Impressionism: landscape conceived simply as an optical phenomenon, so that a man in it has no greater value than a bush. The cubist and abstract painters went still further by eliminating the third dimension, which, inevitably, divided a painting into planes of varying importance.

In music, the same trend toward aesthetic equality of all moments of a composition: Satie, whose simplicity is simply a provocative rejection of inherited musical rhetoric. Debussy, the enchanter, the persecutor of erudite spiders. Janacek doing away with every note that is not indispensable. Stravinsky, who turns away from the Romantic and Classical heritage and seeks his models among the masters of the first half of music history. Webern, who returns to a monothematicism of his own (a twelve-tone one, that is) and achieves a spareness that no one before him could imagine.

And the novel: the questioning of Balzac's famous motto "the novel must compete with the *état civil*" (the state registry of citizens); this questioning is nothing like the bravado of avant-gardists parading their modernness to make it visible to fools; it simply (discreetly) renders pointless (or almost pointless, optional, unimportant) the apparatus for fabricating the illusion of reality. In this regard, a small observation:

If a character is to "compete with the *état civil*," he must start by having a real name. From Balzac to Proust, a character without a name is unthinkable. But Diderot's Jacques has no patronymic and his master has neither first nor family name. Panurge—is that a first or a family name? First names without family names, family names without first names, are not names but *signs*. The protagonist of *The Trial* is not a Josef Kaufmann or Krammer or Kohl, but Josef K. The one in *The Castle* loses even his first name and has to make do with just a letter. Broch's *The Guiltless*: one of the protagonists is designated by the letter A. In *The Sleepwalkers*, Esch and Huguenau have no first names. Ulrich, the protagonist of *The Man Without Qualities*, has no family name. Already in my early stories, by instinct, I avoided naming the characters. In *Life Is Elsewhere*, the hero has only a first name, his mother is known only by the term "Mama," his girlfriend as "the redhead," and her lover as "the man in his forties." Was that mannerism? At the time, I was operating with a total spontaneity whose meaning I understood only later: I was obeying the aesthetic of the "third (or overtime) period": I did not want to make readers think my characters are real and have an official family record.

10

Thomas Mann: *The Magic Mountain*. The very long passages of data on the characters, on their pasts, their way of dressing, their way of speaking (with all the language tics), etc.; very detailed description of sanatorium life; description of the historical moment (the years just preceding the 1914 war), for example, the social customs of the time: the recently discovered passion for photography, a chocolate craze, sketching blindfolded, Esperanto, solitaire, phonograph listening, spiritualist séances (a true novelist, Mann characterizes an era by practices soon to be abandoned and that ordinary historiography misses). The very prolix dialogue reveals its informative function whenever it departs from the few principal themes, and in Mann even dreams are descriptions: after his first day in the sanatorium, the young hero, Hans Castorp, falls asleep; in his thoroughly commonplace dream, all the day's events recur in faintly distorted form. This is very far from Breton, for whom dream is the wellspring of a released imagination. Here the dream has one function only: to make the reader familiar with the milieu, to confirm his illusion of reality.

Thus a vast *background* is meticulously depicted, before which are played out Hans Castorp's fate and the ideological duel between two consumptives: Settembrini and Naphta; the one a Freemason and democrat, the other a Jesuit and autocrat, both of them incurably ill. Mann's tranquil irony relativizes these two learned men's truths; their dispute has no winner. But the novel's irony goes further and reaches its pinnacle in the scene where, each surrounded by his little audience and intoxicated by his own implacable logic, they both push their arguments to the extreme so that no one can any longer tell who stands for progress and who for tradition, who for reason and who for the irrational, who for the spirit and who for the body. Over several pages we witness an enormous confusion where words lose their meaning, and the debate is all the more violent because the positions are interchangeable. Some two hundred pages later, at the end of the novel (the war is soon to break out), all the patients in the sanatorium fall into a state of irrational irritability, inexplicable hatreds; then Settembrini insults Naphta and the two invalids go off to fight a duel that will end in the suicide of one of them; and suddenly we understand that what sets men against one another is not irreconcilable ideological antagonism but an aggressivity beyond the rational, an obscure, unexplained force for which ideas are merely a screen, a mask, a pretext. Thus this magnificent "novel of ideas" is at the same time (especially for a reader at the end of our century) a dreadful requestioning of ideas as such, a great farewell to the era that believed in ideas and in their power to run the world.

Mann and Musil. Despite the closeness of their birth dates, their aesthetics belong to two different eras in the novel's history. Both are novelists of immense intellectuality. In the Mann novel, the intellectuality shows mainly in the dialogues about ideas carried on before the backdrop of a *descriptive novel*. In *The Man Without Qualities*, the intellectuality is manifest at every instant, thoroughgoing; as against Mann's descriptive novel, Musil's is a *thinking novel*. Here too the events are set in a concrete milieu (Vienna) and in a concrete moment (the same one as in *The Magic Mountain*: just before the 1914 war), but whereas in Mann Davos is described in detail, in Musil Vienna is barely named, the author not even deigning to evoke the look of its streets, its squares, its parks (it simply disregards that "apparatus for fabricating the illusion of reality"). We are in the Austro-Hungarian Empire, but it is systematically called by a derisive sobriquet: Kakania. Kakania: the Empire deconcretized, generalized, reduced to a few basic situations, the Empire transformed into an ironical replica of the Empire. This Kakania is not a *background* to the novel as Davos is in Thomas Mann, it is one of the novel's very *themes*; it is not described, it is analyzed and thought through.

Mann explained that the structure of *The Magic Mountain* is musical, built out of themes that are developed as in a symphony, that return, that intersect, that accompany the novel throughout. This is true, but it should be noted that a theme does not signify quite the same thing in Mann and in Musil. To start with, in Mann the themes (time, the body, illness, death, etc.) are developed in front of a vast *nonthematic background* (descriptions of place, time, customs, people) more or less as the themes of a sonata are enveloped in music that is other than the theme—the bridges and the transitions. Then also, his themes are strongly *"polyhistorical"* (i.e., multidisciplinary) in nature, that is to say: Mann makes use of every means offered by the various branches of knowledge—sociology, political science, medicine, botany, physics, chemistry—to illuminate this or that theme; as though he hoped by this popularization of knowledge to create a solid didactic base for analyzing themes; to my mind, too often and for overlong stretches, this diverts his novel from the essential—for let us remember, the essential for a novel is what only a novel can say.

In Musil, theme analysis is another matter: first, it has nothing multidisciplinary to it; the novelist doesn't set up as a scholar, a doctor, a sociologist, a historian, he analyzes *human situations* that are not part of some scientific field but are simply part of life. This is how Broch and Musil saw the historical task for the novel after the era of psychological realism: if European philosophy could not think out man's life, think out his "concrete metaphysics," then it is the novel that is fated finally to take over this vacant terrain where nothing could ever replace it (existential philosophy has confirmed this by a negative proof; for the analysis of existence cannot become a system; existence cannot be systematized, and Heidegger, a poetry lover, was wrong to disregard the history of the novel, for it contains the greatest treasury of existential wisdom).

Second, as opposed to Mann, in Musil *everything becomes theme* (existential questioning). If everything becomes theme, the background disappears and, as in a cubist painting, there is nothing but foreground. It is this abolition of the background that I consider to be the structural revolution Musil brought about. Great changes often have an unobtrusive appearance. Indeed, its lengthy reflections, the slow tempo of its sentences, give *The Man Without Qualities* the feel of "traditional" writing. No overturning of chronology. No interior monologues à la Joyce. No abolishing of punctuation. No annihilating of character or action. For some two thousand pages, we follow the modest

story of a young intellectual, Ulrich, who visits several
mistresses, meets with some friends, and works for an
organization as sober as it is grotesque (this is where
the novel, almost imperceptibly, moves away from the
plausible and turns into play), whose purpose is to
arrange the emperor's anniversary celebration, a great
"festival of peace" planned (and this is a comic bomb
slipped under the book's foundation) for the year
1918. Each little situation is as if frozen in its tracks
(this oddly slowed tempo is where Musil occasionally
recalls Joyce), to be pierced by a long gaze that considers what it means, how to understand it and think it
through.

In *The Magic Mountain*, Mann transformed the
several years before the 1914 war into a magnificent
farewell party for the nineteenth century, gone forever.
The Man Without Qualities, set in the same years,
examines the human situations of the time to come: of
that *terminal period* of the Modern Era that began in
1914 and, it seems, is in the process of ending today
before our eyes. Actually, everything is there already in
the Musil Kakania: the reign of a runaway technology
that turns people into statistics (the novel opens on a
street where an accident has occurred; a man is lying
on the ground and a couple of passersby comment on
the event by citing the annual number of traffic acci-
dents); speed as the supreme value of a world intoxicated by technology; opaque and pervasive bureaucracy (Musil's offices are a great match to Kafka's);
the comical sterility of ideologies that understand
nothing, that provide no guidance (the glorious age of
Settembrini and Naphta is finished); journalism, the
heir to what used to be called culture; modernity's col-

laborationists; solidarity with criminals as the mystical expression of the human rights religion (the characters Clarisse and Moosbrugger); infantophilia and infantocracy (Hans Sepp, a fascist before the term was born, whose ideology is based on adoration of the child in us).

11

When I finished *Farewell Waltz*, at the very start of the 1970s, I considered my career as a writer over. It was under the Russian occupation and my wife and I had other worries. It wasn't until we had been in France a year (and thanks to France) that, after six years of a total interruption, I began without passion to write again. Feeling intimidated, and to regain my footing, I decided to tie into something I had already done: to write a kind of second volume of *Laughable Loves*. What a regression! Those short stories had started me on my way as a writer twenty years before. Fortunately, after drafting two or three of these "Laughable Loves II," I saw that I was writing an entirely different thing: not a story collection but a novel (later entitled *The Book of Laughter and Forgetting*), a novel in seven parts that were independent yet so closely bound that any one of them read by itself would lose much of its meaning.

At once, whatever mistrust I still harbored toward the art of the novel disappeared: by giving each part the nature of a short story, I made unnecessary the whole seemingly unavoidable technique of large-scale novel composition. In my project I happened upon the old *Chopin strategy*, the strategy of *small-scale composition* that has no need of nonthematic passages. (Does that mean that the story is the small form of the novel? Yes. There is no ontological difference between story and novel, as there is between the novel and poetry or the novel and theater.) How are these seven small, independent compositions related if they have no action in common? All that holds them together, that makes them a novel, is that they treat the same themes. As I worked I thus came across another old strategy: *Beethoven's variation strategy*; this allowed me to stay in direct, uninterrupted contact with some existential questions that fascinate me and that this novel in variation form explores from multiple angles in sequence.

This sequential exploration of themes has a logic, and it determines the linkage of the parts. For example: Part One ("Lost Letters") introduces the theme of man and history in its basic version: man collides with history and it crushes him. In Part Two ("Mama") this theme is turned around: for Mama, the arrival of the Russian tanks is a small matter compared to the pears in her garden ("tanks are perishable, pears are eternal"). Part Six ("The Angels"), in which the heroine, Tamina, drowns, would seem to be the tragic conclusion of the novel; yet the novel doesn't end there but ends in the next part, which is neither poignant nor dramatic nor tragic; it recounts the erotic life of a new character, Jan. The history theme appears here briefly and for the last time: "Jan had friends who like him had left their old homeland and who devoted all their time to the struggle for its lost freedom. All of them had sometimes felt that the bond tying them to their country was just an illusion and that only enduring habit kept them prepared to die for something they did not care about"; this touches on that metaphysical *border* (border: another theme worked out in the course of the novel) beyond which everything loses its meaning. The island where Tamina's tragic life ends is dominated by the *laughter* (another theme) of the angels, while Part Seven echoes with "the devil's laughter," which turns everything (everything: history, sex, tragedies) into smoke. Only then does the trail of themes draw toward an end, and the book can close.

12

In the six books of his maturity (*The Dawn*; *Human, All Too Human*; *The Gay Science*; *Beyond Good and Evil*; *Toward a Genealogy of Morals*; *The Twilight of the Idols*), Nietzsche is always pursuing, developing, elaborating, affirming, refining the same compositional archetype. Its principles: the basic unit of the book is the chapter; its length ranges from a single sentence to many pages; without exception the chapters consist of a single paragraph; they are always numbered; in *Human, All Too Human* and in *The Gay Science*, they are numbered and given titles besides. A certain number of chapters make up a part, and a certain number of parts, a book. The book is built on a principal theme, which is specified by the title (beyond good and evil, the gay science, a genealogy of morals, etc.); the various parts treat themes derived from the principal theme (such parts being either titled, as in *Human, All Too Human*, *Beyond Good and Evil*, *The Twilight of the Idols*, or else merely numbered). Certain of these derived themes are arranged vertically (in which each part discusses mainly the theme set out by the part's title), whereas others run horizontally through the entire book. This makes for a composition that is at once maximally articulated (divided into many fairly autonomous units) and maximally unified (the same themes constantly recur). It also makes for a composition imbued with an extraordinary sense of rhythm based on the alternation of short and long chapters: for instance, the fourth part of *Beyond Good and Evil* consists exclusively of very short aphorisms (like a kind of divertissement or scherzo). But above all: this is a composition where there is no need for filler, for transitions, for weak passages, and where the tension never slackens because all we get is thoughts speeding toward us "from outside, from above or below, like events or thunderbolts."

13

If a philosopher's thought is so thoroughly bound up with the formal organization of his text, can it exist outside that text? Can Nietzsche's thought be extracted from Nietzsche's prose? Certainly not. Thought, expression, composition are inseparable. Is what is valid for Nietzsche valid in general? That is: can we say that the thought (the meaning) of a work is always, and by principle, inseparable from its composition?

Oddly, no, we cannot say that. In music, for a long time a composer's originality consisted exclusively in his melodic-harmonic inventiveness, which he set out, so to speak, in compositional schemes that were not determined by him but were more or less preestablished: masses, Baroque suites, Baroque concertos, etc. Their various sections were arranged according to an order determined by tradition, so that, for instance, with clocklike regularity, suites always ended with a fast dance, and so on.

Beethoven's thirty-two piano sonatas, which cover nearly his whole creative life, from the age of twenty-five to fifty-two, represent an immense evolution during which sonata composition is completely transformed. The earliest sonatas still do not go beyond Haydn and Mozart's compositional thinking: four movements; *allegro* in sonata form; *lied* in a slow tempo; *minuet* or *scherzo* in a faster tempo; *rondo* in a rapid tempo.

The disadvantages of such composition are immediately apparent: the most important, most dramatic, longest movement is the first; the sequence of movements is thus a devolution: from the gravest to the lightest; moreover, until Beethoven, the sonata was still midway between a collection of pieces (at the time, separate movements were often played at concerts) and an indivisible, unitary composition. As his thirty-two sonatas evolved, Beethoven gradually replaced the old composition scheme with one that was more concentrated (often reduced to three or even two movements), more dramatic (the center of gravity shifts to the final movement), more unified (mainly by a consistent emotional mood). But the real meaning of this evolution (which made it actually a *revolution*) lay not in replacing an unsatisfactory scheme with another, better one but in *shattering the very principle of the preestablished composition scheme*.

Indeed, that general compliance with the sonata's or the symphony's prescribed scheme is somewhat ridiculous. Imagine all the great symphonists, including Haydn and Mozart, Schumann and Brahms, weeping in their *adagios* and then turning into little children when the last movement starts, darting into the schoolyard to dance, hop, and holler that all's well that ends well. This is what we might call "the stupidity of music." Beethoven saw that the only way to get around it is to *make composition radically individual*.

This idea is the first item in his artistic testament addressed to all the arts, to all artists, and which I shall state thus: the composition (the architectural organization of a work) should not be seen as some preexistent matrix, loaned to an author for him to fill out with his invention; the composition should itself be an invention, an invention that engages all the author's originality.

I cannot say how thoroughly this message was heard and understood. But Beethoven did draw all of its implications—magnificently—in his last sonatas, each of them composed in a manner unique and unprecedented.

14

The sonata Opus 111; it has only two movements: the first, which is dramatic, is worked out more or less classically in sonata form; the second, meditative in character, is written in variation form (a form rather unusual in sonatas before Beethoven): there is no play of contrasts and differences among the individual variations, only an intensification that keeps adding fresh nuance to the previous variation and gives this long movement an exceptional unity of tone.

The more thoroughly unified each of the movements, the greater its difference from the other. Disproportionate in length: the first movement (in Schnabel's recording): 8:14; the second: 17:42. The second half of the sonata is thus more than twice as long as the first (a case without precedent in the history of the sonata)! Furthermore: the first movement is dramatic, the second calm, reflective. Now, to begin dramatically and end with so lengthy a meditation would seem to contradict every architectural principle and condemn the sonata to the loss of all the dramatic tension previously so dear to Beethoven.

But it is just that unexpected juxtaposition of these two movements that is eloquent, that speaks, that becomes the *semantic gesture* of the sonata, its metaphorical sense evoking the image of a hard, short life and the endless yearning song that follows it. That metaphorical sense, beyond the power of words to grasp and yet strong and insistent, gives the two movements a unity. An inimitable unity. (The impersonal composition of a Mozart sonata could be imitated endlessly; the composition of the sonata Opus 111 is so personal that imitating it would be forgery.)

Opus 111 makes me think of Faulkner's *The Wild Palms*. In it a love story alternates with the story of an escaped convict, two stories that have nothing in common, no character nor even any discernible kinship of motifs or themes. A composition that cannot serve as a model for any other novelist; that can exist only once; that is arbitrary, inadvisable, unjustifiable; unjustifiable because behind it can be heard an *es muss sein* that makes any justification superfluous.

15

By his refusal of systems, Nietzsche brought deep changes to the way philosophy is done: as Hannah Arendt defined it, Nietzsche's thought is *experimental thought*. His first impulse is to break up whatever is rigid, to undermine commonly accepted systems, to open rifts for venturing into the unknown; the philosopher of the future will be an *experimenter*, Nietzsche said; free to go off in various directions that could, conceivably, come into conflict.

Although I favor a strong presence of thought in the novel, this is not to say that I like the so-called philosophical novel, that subjugation of the novel to a philosophy, that "tale-making" out of moral or political ideas. Authentically novelistic thought (as the novel has known it since Rabelais) is always unsystematic; undisciplined; it is similar to Nietzsche's; it is experimental; it forces rifts in all the idea systems that surround us; it explores (particularly through its characters) all lines of thought by trying to follow each of them to its end. And there is this too about systematic thought: a person who thinks is automatically prompted to systematize; it is his eternal temptation (mine too, even in writing this book): a temptation to describe all the implications of his ideas; to preempt any objections and refute them in advance; thus to barricade his ideas. Now, a person who thinks should not try to persuade others of his belief; that is what puts him on the road to a system; on the lamentable road of the "man of conviction"; politicians like to call themselves that; but what is a conviction? it is a thought that has come to a stop, that has congealed, and the "man of conviction" is a man restricted; experimental thought seeks not to persuade but to inspire; to inspire another thought, to set thought moving; that is why a novelist must systematically desystematize his thought, kick at the barricade that he himself has erected around his ideas.

16

Nietzsche's refusal of systematic thought has another consequence: an immense *broadening of theme*; the barriers between the various philosophical disciplines, which have kept the real world from being seen in its full range, are fallen, and from then on everything human can become the object of a philosopher's thought. That too brings philosophy nearer to the novel: for the first time philosophy is pondering not epistemology, not aesthetics or ethics, the phenomenology of mind or the critique of reason, etc., but *everything human*.

In expounding Nietzsche's philosophy, historians or professors do not merely reduce it—that of course—but also distort it by turning it into its opposite, namely into a system. Is there still room in their systematized Nietzsche for his thoughts on women, on the Germans, on Europe, on Bizet, on Goethe, on Victor Hugo-style kitsch, on Aristophanes, on lightness of style, on boredom, on play, on translation, on the spirit of obedience, on possession of the other and on all the psychological forms of such possession, on the savants and their mental limitations, on the *Schauspieler*, actors on history's stage—is there still room for a thousand psychological observations that can be found nowhere else, except perhaps in a few rare novelists?

As Nietzsche brought philosophy closer to the novel, so Musil brought the novel toward philosophy. This rapprochement doesn't mean that Musil is less a novelist than other novelists. Just as Nietzsche is no less a philosopher than other philosophers.

Musil's *thinking novel* too brought about an unprecedented broadening of theme; nothing that can be thought about is henceforth excluded from the art of the novel.

17

When I was thirteen or fourteen years old, I used to take lessons in musical composition. Not because I was a child prodigy but because of my father's quiet tact. It was during the war, and a friend of his, a Jewish composer, was required to wear the yellow star; people had begun to avoid him. Not knowing how to declare his solidarity, my father thought of asking him just then to give me lessons. They were confiscating Jewish apartments, and the composer kept having to move on to smaller and smaller places, ending up, just before he left for Theresienstadt, in a little flat where many people were camping, crammed, in every room. All along, he had held on to the small piano on which I would play my harmony or counterpoint exercises while strangers went about their business around us.

Of all this I retain only my admiration for him, and three or four images. Especially this one: seeing me out after a lesson, he stopped by the door and suddenly said to me: "There are many surprisingly weak passages in Beethoven. But it is the weak passages that bring out the strong ones. It's like a lawn—if it weren't there, we couldn't enjoy the beautiful tree growing on it."

A peculiar idea. That it has stayed in my memory is even more peculiar. Maybe I felt honored at getting to hear a confidential admission from the teacher, a secret, a great trick of the trade that only the initiated are permitted to know.

Whatever it was, that brief remark from my teacher of the time has haunted me all my life (I have defended it, now I dispute it, but I have never doubted its importance); without it, this text could very certainly not have been written.

But dearer to me than that remark in itself is the image of a man who, a while before his hideous journey, stood thinking aloud, in front of a child, about the problem of composing a work of art.

PART SEVEN

The Unloved Child of the Family

I've referred many times to Leos Janacek's music. It is well known in England and the U.S.A., and in Germany. But in France? In the other Romance-language countries? And which of his works could be known? On February 15, 1992, I go to a large record shop in Paris to see what is available.

1

I immediately find *Taras Bulba* (1918) and the Sinfonietta (1926): the orchestral works of his *great period*; as the most popular works (the most accessible to the average music lover), they are almost always put together on the same disc.

The Suite for String Orchestra (1877), the "Idyll" for String Orchestra (1878), and the *Lachian Dances* (1890). These are pieces from the *prehistory* of his creative work, whose insignificance astonishes people expecting Janacek's name to mean great music.

I pause at the terms "prehistory" and "great period":
Janacek was born in 1854. That is the whole paradox. This great figure of modern music is older than
the last of the great Romantic composers: four years
older than Puccini, six years older than Mahler, ten
years older than Richard Strauss. For a long time he
wrote works that, because of his allergy to the excesses
of Romanticism, are notable only for their pronounced
traditionalism. Always dissatisfied, he punctuated his
life with torn-up scores; only at the turn of the century
did he arrive at his own style. In the twenties, his compositions appeared on modern-music concert programs
alongside Stravinsky, Bartók, and Hindemith; but he
was thirty, forty years older than they. A solitary conservative in his youth, he became an innovator when
he was old. But he was still alone. For though he stood
with the great modernists, he was different from them.
He came to his style without them, his modernism had
a different nature, a different genesis, different roots.

2

I continue my stroll among the bins at the record shop;
with no trouble I find the two String Quartets (1924,
1928): this is Janacek's peak; all his *expressionism* is
concentrated here in total perfection. Five recordings,
all excellent. Even so, I regret not finding (I've long
been looking for it on compact disc) the most authentic
(and still the best) performance of these quartets, that
of the Janacek Quartet (the old Supraphon recording
[50556], awarded the Prix de l'Académie Charles-Cros
and the Preis der Deutschen Schallplattenkritik).

I pause at the term "expressionism":

Although he never made the connection himself, Janacek is actually the only great composer to whom the term can be applied fully and in its literal sense: for him, everything is expression, and a note has no right to exist except as expression. Thus the total absence in his work of mere "technique": transitions, developments, the mechanics of contrapuntal filler, routine orchestration (on the contrary, a penchant for previously novel ensembles made up of a few solo instruments), etc. The result for the performer is that, every note being expression, every note (not only every motif, but every note of a motif) must have maximal expressive clarity. Another point: German expressionism is characterized by a predilection for excessive states—delirium, madness. What I'm calling expressionism in Janacek has nothing to do with such one-dimensionality: it is an enormously rich emotional range, a dizzyingly tight, transitionless juxtaposition of tenderness and brutality, fury and peace.

3

I find the beautiful Sonata for Violin and Piano (1921) and the "Fairy Tale" for Violoncello and Piano (1910). *The Diary of a Man Who Disappeared*, for piano, tenor, alto, and three female voices (1919). And then, the works of his very last years; his creativity explodes; never before had he been so free as he was in his seventies, overflowing with humor and invention; the *Glagolitic Mass* (1926), like no other: it is more an orgy than a mass; and it is fascinating. From the same time, the Sextet for Winds (1924), the *Nursery Rhymes* (1927), and two works for piano and various instruments that I especially love despite rarely satisfactory performances: the *Capriccio* (1926) and the Concertino (1925).

I count five recordings of works for piano solo: the Sonata (1905) and two cycles: "On an Overgrown Path" (1902) and "In the Mists" (1912); these beautiful works are always grouped on one disc that is nearly always (unfortunately) filled out by other, minor pieces from his "prehistory." Incidentally, pianists in particular get Janacek wrong, as to both spirit and structure: they nearly all of them succumb to a prettied-up romanticizing: by softening the brutal aspect of this music, by ignoring its *forte* markings and by throwing themselves into the delirium of a nearly systematic *rubato*. (Piano music is particularly undefended against rubato. It is actually difficult to arrange for rhythmic inaccuracy with an orchestra. But the pianist is all by himself. His fearsome soul can rampage with no control and no constraint.)

I pause at the term "romanticize":

Janacek's expressionism is not an exaggerated extension of Romantic sentimentality. On the contrary, it is one historical option for moving out of Romanticism. An option very different from the one Stravinsky chose: unlike him, Janacek did not reproach the Romantics for having talked about feelings; he reproached them for having falsified them; for having substituted sentimental gesticulation ("a Romantic lie," René Girard* calls it) for the unmedi-

---

*At last, an occasion to cite René Girard; his *Mensonge romantique et vérité romanesque* is the best book I have ever read on the art of the novel.

ated truth of the emotions. He has a passion for the passions, but still more for the precision he musters to express them. Stendhal, not Hugo. Which involves breaking away from Romantic music, from its spirit, from its hypertrophied sonorities (Janacek's economy of sound shocked everyone in his time), from its structure.

4

I pause at the term "structure":

—whereas Romantic music sought to impose emotional unity on a given movement, Janacek's musical structure is based on unusually frequent alternations of different, even contradictory, emotional fragments within a single piece, a single movement;

—corresponding to this emotional diversity is a diversity of tempi and meters, which also alternate unusually often;

—the coexistence of many contradictory emotions in a very limited space makes for a semantics that is brand new (what astonishes and fascinates is the *unexpected juxtaposition of emotions*). The coexistence of emotions is horizontal (they follow one another) but also (even more unusual) vertical (they sound simultaneously as a *polyphony of emotions*). For example: at the same time, we hear a nostalgic melody, beneath it a furious ostinato motif, and above it another melody, which sounds like cries. If the performer doesn't understand that all these lines have equal semantic importance and that therefore none of them should be made into mere accompaniment, into an impressionistic murmur, he is missing the structure characteristic of Janacek's music.

The permanent coexistence of contradictory emotions gives Janacek's music its *dramatic* quality; dramatic in the most literal sense of the term: this music does not evoke a narrator telling a tale; rather, it evokes a stage set on which many different characters are *simultaneously* present, speaking, confronting each other; the seed of this *dramatic space* is often to be found within a single melodic motif. As in the first measures of the Piano Sonata:

The forte motif of sixteenth notes in the fourth measure, still part of the melodic theme developed in the preceding measures (it consists of the same intervals), at the same time forms its harsh emotional opposite. Some measures later, we see how much the brutality of this "secessionist" motif contradicts the elegiac melody it comes from:

In the following measure, the two melodies, the original and the "secessionist," come together; not in an emotional harmony, but in a contradictory polyphony of the emotions, the way yearning tears and rebellion can come together:

In their desire to lay an emotional uniformity on these measures, all the pianists whose recordings I could find at the record shop neglect the sudden *forte* Janacek marked in the fourth measure; thus they strip the "secessionist" motif of its brutal character and Janacek's music of all of the inimitable tension that makes it recognizable (if it is properly understood) instantly, from its very first notes.

5

The operas: I don't find *The Excursions of Mr. Broucek* in the record bins and I don't miss it, as I consider this work rather a failure; all the others are here, conducted by Sir Charles Mackerras: *Destiny* (written in 1904, whose versified, catastrophically naïve libretto and even its music, coming after *Jenufa*, represent a distinct regression); then five masterpieces that I admire unreservedly: *Katia Kabanova*, *The Cunning Little Vixen*, *The Makropulos Affair*; and *Jenufa*: Sir Charles Mackerras has the immeasurable merit of having finally (in 1982, after sixty-six years!) rid that opera of the arrangement that was imposed on it in Prague in 1916. Still more brilliant a success, I think, is his revision of the score of *From the House of the Dead*. Thanks to Mackerras, we became aware (in 1980, after fifty-two years!) how much the adapters' arrangements had weakened this opera. Restored to its original form, wherein it regained all its spare and strange sonority (poles apart from Romantic symphonism), *From the House of the Dead* emerges alongside Berg's *Wozzeck* as the truest, the greatest opera of our dark century.

6

An insoluble practical difficulty: in Janacek's operas, the charm of the vocal parts does not lie only in the beauty of the melodies but lies also in the psychological meaning (always an unexpected meaning) that the melody confers not on a scene as a whole but on each phrase, each word sung. But how to sing it in Berlin or in Paris? In Czech (Mackerras's solution), the listener will hear only meaningless syllables, gain no understanding of the psychological subtleties present at every melodic turn. In translation, then, as was done when these operas started their international career? That too is problematic: the French language, for example, would not tolerate the stress put on the first syllable of Czech words, and in French the intonation would take on an entirely different psychological meaning.

(There is something poignant if not tragic in the fact that Janacek should have concentrated most of his innovative powers on opera of all things, thus putting himself at the mercy of the most conservative bourgeois audience imaginable. Moreover: his originality lies in an unprecedented revaluation of the sung *word*, meaning specifically the Czech word, which is incomprehensible in ninety-nine percent of the theaters in the world. It's difficult to imagine a greater self-imposed accumulation of obstacles. His operas are the most beautiful homage ever paid the Czech language. Homage? Yes. Homage in the shape of a sacrifice. He *immolated* his universal music on the altar of a nearly unknown language.)

7

A question: If music is a supranational language, is the semantics of speech intonations also supranational in nature? Or not at all? Or at least to some degree? Problems that fascinated Janacek. So much so that in his last will and testament he bequeathed nearly all his money to the University of Brno to underwrite research in the musical aspect of spoken language (its rhythms, its intonations, its semantics). But as we know, people don't give a damn about wills and testaments.

8

Sir Charles Mackerras's admirable fidelity to Janacek's work means: grasping and defending what is essential. Aiming for the essential is, indeed, Janacek's artistic ethic; its rule being: only absolutely necessary (semantically necessary) notes have a right to exist; from which follows an extreme spareness in orchestration. By ridding the scores of their imposed additions, Mackerras restored that spareness and thus made clearer the Janacek aesthetic.

But there is also another, an opposite, kind of fidelity that takes the form of a passion to collect everything an author leaves behind him. Since in his lifetime every author has already tried to make public everything essential, the *garbage-can scavengers* are devotees of the unessential.

A perfect example of the scavenger spirit shows in the recording of the pieces for piano and violin or cello (ADDA 581136/37). On this two-disc set, minor or worthless pieces (folk music transcriptions, abandoned variants, juvenilia, sketches) take up some fifty minutes—a third of the time—and are scattered among the full-scale compositions. For example, there is six and a half minutes of music written to accompany gymnastic exercises. O composers, control yourselves when pretty ladies from a gym come to ask a little favor! Your good turn will outlive you—as a laughing-stock!

9

I go on looking through the bins. I search in vain for certain beautiful orchestral works of Janacek's mature years ("The Fiddler's Child," 1912; "The Ballad of Blanik," 1920), his cantatas (especially: *Amarus*, 1898), and some compositions from the time when his style was taking shape, works notable for their moving and unparalleled simplicity: *Pater Noster* (1901), *Ave Maria* (1904). The most important and serious lack here is his choral works; for in our century there is nothing in this genre to equal the four masterpieces of Janacek's great period: "Marycka Magdonova" (1906), "Schoolmaster Halfar" (1906), "The Seventy Thousand" (1909), "The Wandering Madman" (1922): works of diabolic technical difficulty, they were excellently performed in Czechoslovakia; those recordings must surely exist on old pressings from the Czech firm Supraphon, but for years now these have been impossible to find.

10

The balance sheet, then, is not entirely bad, but it is not good either. With Janacek this was so from the beginning. *Jenufa* reached the world's stages twenty years after it was written. Too late. For after twenty years the polemical character of an aesthetic disappears, and then its novelty is no longer discernible. That is why Janacek's music is so often badly understood, and so badly performed; its historic meaning is blurred; it seems unclassifiable; like a beautiful garden laid out just next door to History; the question of its place in the evolution (better: in the genesis) of modern music doesn't even arise.

If in the case of Broch, of Musil, of Gombrowicz, and in a certain sense of Bartók, their recognition was delayed by historic catastrophes (Nazism, war), in Janacek's case it was his small nation that completely took over the role of the catastrophes.

11

Small nations. The concept is not quantitative; it describes a situation; a destiny: small nations haven't the comfortable sense of being there always, past and future; they have all, at some point or another in their history, passed through the antechamber of death; always faced with the arrogant ignorance of the large nations, they see their existence perpetually threatened or called into question; for their very existence *is* a question.

Most of the small European nations became free and independent in the nineteenth and twentieth centuries. Thus they have their own evolutionary rhythm. For the arts, this historical asynchrony has often been a fruitful thing, as it made for the curious telescoping of different eras: for instance, Janacek and Bartók were both ardent participants in the national struggle of their peoples; that is their nineteenth-century side: an extraordinary sense of reality, an attachment to the working classes and to popular arts, a more spontaneous rapport with the audience; these qualities, already gone from the arts in the large countries, here merged with the aesthetic of modernism in a surprising, inimitable, felicitous marriage.

The small nations form "another Europe," whose evolution runs in counterpoint with that of the large nations. An observer can be fascinated by the often astonishing intensity of their cultural life. This is the advantage of smallness: the wealth in cultural events is on a "human scale"; everyone can encompass that wealth, can participate in the totality of cultural life; this is why, in its best moments, a small nation can bring to mind life in an ancient Greek city.

That potential for everyone's participation in everything can also bring to mind something else: the family; a small nation resembles a big family and likes to describe itself that way. In the language of the smallest European people, in Icelandic, the term for "family" is *fjölskylda*; the etymology is eloquent: *skylda* means "obligation"; *fjöl* means "multiple." Family is thus "a multiple obligation." Icelanders have a single word for "family ties": *fjölskyldubönd*: "the cords (*bönd*) of multiple obligations." Thus in the big family that is a small country, the artist is bound in multiple ways, by multiple cords. When Nietzsche noisily savaged the German character, when Stendhal announced that he preferred Italy to his homeland, no German or Frenchman took offense; if a Greek or a Czech dared to say the same thing, his family would curse him as a detestable traitor.

Secluded behind their inaccessible languages, the small European nations (their life, their history, their culture) are very ill known; people think, naturally enough, that this is the principal handicap to international recognition of their art. But it is the reverse: what handicaps their art is that everything and everyone (critics, historians, compatriots as well as foreigners) hooks the art onto the great national family portrait photo and will not let it get away. Gombrowicz: to no purpose (and with no competence either), foreign commentators struggle to explain his work by discoursing on the Polish nobility, on the Polish Baroque, etc., etc. As Lakis Proguidis writes,* they "Polonize"

---

*Lakis Proguidis, *Un écrivain malgré la critique* (Paris: Gallimard, 1989).

him, "re-Polonize" him, push him back into the *small context* of the national. However, it is not familiarity with the Polish nobility but familiarity with the international modern novel (that is, with the *large context*) that will bring us to understand the originality and, hence, the value of Gombrowicz's novels.

12

Ah, small nations. Within that warm intimacy, each envies each, everyone watches everyone. "Families, I hate you!" And still another line from Gide: "There is nothing more dangerous for you than *your own* family, *your own* room, *your own* past. . . . You must leave them." Ibsen, Strindberg, Joyce, Seferis knew this. They spent a large part of their lives abroad, away from the family's power. For Janacek, that ingenuous patriot, this was inconceivable. And he paid the price.

Of course, all modern artists have had experience with hatred and incomprehension from the public; but they were also surrounded by disciples, by theoreticians, by performers who from the beginning were defending them and promulgating the authentic idea of their art. In Brno, in a province where he spent his whole life, Janacek too had his faithful followers, some performers who were often admirable (the Janacek Quartet was among the last heirs to this tradition) but whose influence was weak. From the early years of the century, official Czech musicology disdained him. Knowing no other musical gods but Smetana, nor other laws than the Smetanesque, the national ideologues were irritated by his otherness. The pope of

Prague musicology, Professor Nejedly, who late in his life, in 1948, became minister and omnipotent ruler of culture in Stalinized Czechoslovakia, took with him into his bellicose senility only two great passions: Smetana worship and Janacek vilification. The most useful support of Janacek's lifetime came from Max Brod; between 1918 and 1928 Brod translated all Janacek's operas into German, thereby opening frontiers to them and delivering them from the exclusive power of the jealous family. In 1924 he wrote the first monograph on Janacek; but Brod was not Czech, and thus the first Janacek monograph was in German. The second was in French, published in Paris in 1930. The first complete monograph in Czech only appeared thirty-nine years after Brod's.[*] Franz Kafka compared Brod's campaign for Janacek to the one for Dreyfus earlier—a startling comparison that indicates the degree of hostility leveled at Janacek in his own country. From 1903 to 1916, the National Theater of Prague persistently turned away his first opera, *Jenufa*. In Dublin at the same time, from 1905 to 1914, Joyce's countrymen refused publication of his first book of prose, *Dubliners*, in 1912 even burning the proofs. Janacek's story differs from Joyce's in the perversity of its outcome: he was forced to see the pre-

---

[*]Jaroslav Vogel, *Leos Janacek* (Prague, 1963; revised English translation, New York: W. W. Norton, 1981), a detailed and honest book, but limited in its judgments by its national and nationalistic horizon. Bartók and Berg, the two composers most closely related to Janacek on the international scene: the former is not mentioned at all, the latter barely. How is one to locate Janacek on the map of modern music without these two reference points?

miere of *Jenufa* directed by the conductor who for fourteen years had dismissed him, who for fourteen years had had only contempt for his music. He was obliged to be grateful. After that humiliating victory (the score was reddened with corrections, deletions, additions), he eventually came to be tolerated in Bohemia. I say "tolerated." If a family doesn't succeed in annihilating its unloved son, it humiliates him with maternal indulgence. The common view in Bohemia, meant as favorable, tears him out of the context of modern music and immures him in local concerns: passion for folklore, Moravian patriotism, admiration for Woman, for Nature, for Russia, for Slavitude, and other nonsense. Family, I hate you. Not a single important musicological study analyzing the *aesthetic newness* of his work has to this day been written by any of his compatriots. There is no significant school of Janacek interpretation, which might have made his strange aesthetic intelligible to the world. No strategy for making his music known. No complete recorded edition of his works. No complete edition of his theoretical and critical writings.

And yet that little nation has never had any artist greater than he.

13

Let us go on. I consider the last decade of his life: his country independent, his music at last applauded, himself loved by a young woman; his works become more and more bold, free, merry. A Picasso-like old age. In the summer of 1928, his beloved and her child come to see him in his little country house. The boy wanders off into the forest, the old man goes looking for him, runs every which way, catches cold and develops pneumonia, is taken to the hospital, and, a few days later, dies. She is there with him. From the time I was fourteen, I have heard the gossip that he died making love on his hospital bed. Not very plausible but, as Hemingway liked to say, truer than the truth. What better way to crown the wild euphoria that was his last years?

And it is also proof that within his national family there were, after all, people who loved him. For that legend is a bouquet set upon his grave.

PART EIGHT

Paths in the Fog

What Is Irony?

In Part Four of *The Book of Laughter and Forgetting*,
Tamina, the heroine, needs some help from her friend
Bibi, a young graphomaniac; to win her goodwill, she
arranges for her to meet a local writer named Banaka.
He explains to the graphomaniac that today's real
writers have renounced the obsolete art of the novel:
"You know, the novel is the fruit of a human illusion.
The illusion of the power to understand others. But
what do we know of one another? . . . All anyone can
do is give a report on oneself. . . . Anything else is a
lie." And Banaka's friend, a philosophy professor, says:
"Since James Joyce we have known that the greatest
adventure of our lives is the absence of adventure. . . .
Homer's odyssey has been taken inside. It has been
interiorized." Some time after the book appeared, I
found these words as the epigraph to a French novel. I
was very flattered but embarrassed too, because, in my
view, what Banaka and his friend said were just

sophisticated stupidities. At the time, in the seventies, I was hearing them all around me: university chatter cobbled together from scraps of structuralism and psychoanalysis.

This Part Four of *The Book of Laughter and Forgetting* was published in Czechoslovakia as a small, separate volume (the first publication of any work of mine after a twenty-year ban), and a press clipping was sent to me in Paris: the reviewer was pleased with me, and as proof of my intelligence he quoted a line he considered brilliant: "Since James Joyce we have known that the greatest adventure of our lives is the absence of adventure," and so on. I took a strangely wicked pleasure at seeing myself ride back into my native land on a donkey of misunderstanding.

The misapprehension is understandable: I hadn't set out to *ridicule* Banaka and his professor friend. I had not made obvious my reservation about them. On the contrary, I did all I could to conceal it, to give their opinions the elegance of the intellectual discourse that everyone, back then, respected and fervently imitated. If I had made their talk ridiculous, by exaggerating its excesses, I would have produced what is called satire. Satire is a thesis art; sure of its own truth, it ridicules what it determines to combat. The novelist's relation to his characters is never satirical; it is ironic. But how does irony, which is by definition discreet, make itself apparent? By the context: Banaka's and his friend's remarks are set within an environment of gestures, actions, and words that relativize them. The little provincial world that surrounds Tamina is characterized by an innocent egocentrism: everyone has sincere liking for her, and yet no one tries to understand her, not even knowing what "understanding" would mean. When Banaka says that the art of the novel is obsolete because the notion of understanding others is an illusion, he is expressing not only a fashionable aesthetic attitude but, unknowingly, his own misery and that of his milieu: a lack of desire to understand another; an egocentric blindness toward the real world.

Irony means: none of the assertions found in a novel can be taken by itself, each of them stands in a complex and contradictory juxtaposition with other assertions, other situations, other gestures, other ideas, other events. Only a slow reading, twice and many times over, can bring out all the *ironic connections* inside a novel, without which the novel remains uncomprehended.

K.'s Curious Behavior During His Arrest

K. wakes up one morning and, still in bed, rings for his breakfast to be brought. Instead of the maid, two strangers arrive, ordinary men, in ordinary dress, who nevertheless immediately behave with such authority that K. cannot help but feel their force, their power. So although he is exasperated, he is incapable of throwing them out and instead he politely asks them: "Who are you?"

From the beginning, K.'s behavior oscillates between his weakness, prepared to bow to the intruders' unbelievable effrontery (they have come to notify him that he is under arrest), and his fear of appearing ridiculous. For instance, he says firmly: "I shall neither stay here nor let you address me until you have intro-duced yourselves." It would suffice to pull these words out of their ironic setting, to take them literally (as my reader took Banaka's words), and K. would be for us (as he was for Orson Welles in his film version of *The Trial*) a man-in-revolt-against-violence. Yet it suffices to read the text carefully to see that this man said to be in revolt continues to obey the intruders, who not only never deign to introduce themselves but also eat his breakfast and keep him standing the whole time in his nightshirt.

At the end of this scene of odd humiliation (he offers them his hand and they refuse to take it), one of the men says to K.: "You'll be going to the bank now, I suppose?" "To the bank?" asks K. "I thought I was under arrest."

There he is again, the man-in-revolt-against-vio-lence! He is being sarcastic! He is being provocative! As, by the way, Kafka's commentary makes explicit: "K. asked the question with a certain defiance, for though his offer to shake hands had been ignored, he felt, especially now that the inspector had risen to his feet, more and more independent of all these people. He was playing with them. If they should leave, he planned to chase after them to the front door and offer himself up for arrest."

Here is a very subtle irony: K. is capitulating but wants to see himself as someone strong who "plays with them," who mocks them by derisively pretending to take his arrest seriously; he is capitulating but immediately also interprets his capitulation in a way that lets him maintain his dignity in his own eyes.

People first read Kafka with a tragic expression on

their faces. Then they heard that when Kafka read the first chapter of *The Trial* to his friends, he made them all laugh. Thereupon readers started forcing themselves to laugh too, but without knowing exactly why. What actually is so funny in this chapter? K.'s behavior. But what is comic about this behavior?

The question reminds me of the years I spent at the cinema school in Prague. During the teachers' meetings, a friend and I would always watch with a malicious affection one of our colleagues, a writer of about fifty, a man who was subtle and correct but whom we suspected of tremendous, incurable cowardice. We dreamed up the following scenario, which (alas!) we never carried out:

In the middle of the meeting, one of us would suddenly tell him: "On your knees!"

At first he wouldn't understand what we wanted; or more exactly, in his clear-eyed cravenness, he would understand instantly but would think to gain a little time by pretending not to understand.

We would have to say it louder: "On your knees!"

Now he could no longer pretend not to understand. He would be all set to obey, with just one problem: how to do it? How would he get down on his knees here, in front of all of his colleagues, without humiliating himself? He would look desperately for some funny remark to make as he got down: "Will you permit me, my dear colleagues," he would finally say, "to put a cushion under my knees?"

"On your knees and be quiet!"

He'd do it, putting his hands together and slightly tilting his head to the left: "My dear colleagues, if you have really studied Renaissance painting, this is exactly the way Raphael painted Saint Francis of Assisi."

Every day we imagined new variations on this delectable scene, inventing more and more witty remarks for our colleague's efforts to preserve his dignity.

The Second Trial of Josef K.

As opposed to Orson Welles, Kafka's earliest interpreters were far from considering K. an innocent man in revolt against the arbitrary. Max Brod never doubted that Josef K. is guilty. What has he done? According to Brod (*Despair and Salvation in the Work of Franz Kafka* [*Verzweiflung und Erlösung im Werk Franz Kafkas*], 1959), he is guilty of *Lieblosigkeit*, the inability to love. "*Josef K. liebt niemanden, er liebelt nur, deshalb muss er sterben.*" Josef K. loves no one, he only dallies, and therefore he must die. (Let us never forget the sublime stupidity of this sentence!) Brod is quick to adduce two proofs of *Lieblosigkeit*: according to a chapter left unfinished and excluded from *The Trial* (usually published as an appendix), Josef K. has not been to see his mother for three years; he has merely sent her money, getting information about her health from a cousin (a curious resemblance: Meursault, in *The Stranger*, is also accused of not loving his mother). The second piece of evidence is K.'s relationship with Fräulein Bürstner, a relationship that Brod describes as of the "lowest sexuality" (*niedrigster Sexualität*). "Fräulein Bürstner, to whom he is drawn by a kind of desire, remains shadowy to him as a human being, interests him only as a sexual creature."

In his preface to the 1964 Prague edition of *The Trial*, the Czech Kafkologist Eduard Goldstücker criticized K. with equal severity, even though his vocabulary is marked not by theology, like Brod's, but by Marxist-style sociology: "Josef K. is guilty because he has allowed his life to be mechanized, automatized, alienated, to be fitted to the stereotyped rhythm of the social machine, let it be deprived of every human quality; thus K. has broken the law that, according to Kafka, rules all humankind: 'Be human.'" In the fifties Goldstücker underwent a dreadful Stalinist trial where he was accused of imaginary crimes, and he spent four years in prison. I ask myself: how could this man, the victim of a trial himself, some ten years later set up a trial against another defendant, no guiltier than he?

According to Alexandre Vialatte (*L'Histoire secrète du Procès*, 1947), the trial in Kafka's novel is the one that Kafka brings against himself, K. being nothing but his alter ego: Kafka had broken his engagement with Felice, and his future father-in-law "came from Malmö expressly to try the guilty fellow. The hotel room in the Askanischer Hof where this scene unfolded (in July 1914) gave Kafka the sense of a courtroom. . . . He started the next day on 'The Penal Colony' and on *The Trial*. We do not know K.'s crime, and today's morality absolves it. And yet, his 'innocence' is diabolical. . . . In some mysterious way, K. has violated the laws of a mysterious justice that has nothing to do with ours. . . . The judge is Doctor Kafka, the defendant is Doctor Kafka. He pleads guilty to diabolical innocence."

In the first trial (the one Kafka recounts in his novel), the tribunal accuses K. *without specifying the crime*. The Kafkologists were unastonished that a person could be accused without cause and were not spurred to ponder this unheard-of situation, one never examined in any literary work. Instead, they set about playing prosecutor in a new trial that they themselves brought against K., this time trying to figure out the true crime of the accused. Brod: he is incapable of love! Goldstücker: he acquiesced in the mechanization of his life! Vialatte: he broke his engagement! They do deserve credit for one thing: their trial against K. is just as Kafkan as the first one. For if in his first trial K. is accused of *nothing*, in the second he is accused of *no matter what*, which comes to the same because in both cases one thing is clear: K. is guilty not because he has committed a crime but because he has been accused. He is accused, therefore he must die.

Inducing Guilt

There is only one way to understand Kafka's novels: to read them as novels. Rather than search the character K. for a portrait of the author and K.'s words for a mysterious coded message, to pay careful attention to the behavior of the characters, their remarks, their thoughts, and try to imagine them before your eyes. Reading *The Trial* this way, you are immediately struck by K.'s strange reaction to the charge: without having done anything wrong (or without knowing what he did), K. immediately begins to behave as though he is guilty. He feels guilty. He has been made to feel guilty. He has been *culpabilized*.

People used to see a very simple link between

"being guilty" and "feeling guilty": it's the guilty person who feels guilty. In fact, the French word *culpabiliser*—to induce feelings of guilt—is relatively recent; it was first used in 1966 because of psychoanalysis and its innovations in terminology; the noun derived from this verb (*culpabilisation*) was created two years later, in 1968. But long before that, the hitherto unexplored condition of induced guilt feelings was set forth, described, and developed in Kafka's novel, in the character K., and it was shown at different stages of its evolution:

Stage 1: Futile struggle for lost dignity. A man absurdly accused who does not yet doubt his innocence is disturbed to see that he is behaving as if he is guilty. Acting guilty without being so has a humiliating element, which he tries to conceal. Set out in the first scene of the novel, in the next chapter this situation is condensed into a tremendously ironic joke:

An unknown person telephones K.: he is to be interrogated the following Sunday at a house in the suburbs. Without hesitation, he decides to go; out of obedience? out of fear? Oh no, self-delusion works automatically: he wants to go there in order to be done quickly with these nuisances who are wasting his time with their stupid case ("the case was getting under way and he must fight it; this first interrogation must also be the last"). Immediately after, his chief at the bank where he works invites K. to a party on the same Sunday. The invitation is important for K.'s career. Should he therefore ignore the grotesque summons? No; he declines the chief's invitation since, without wanting to acknowledge it to himself, he is already under the sway of the trial.

And so on Sunday he goes to the house. He realizes that the voice on the telephone that gave him the address neglected to specify the hour. No matter; he feels pressed for time, and he *runs* (yes, literally, he runs; in German: *er lief*) across the entire city. He runs in order to arrive on time, even though no hour has been specified. Granted that he has reasons to arrive as early as possible; but in that event, instead of running, why not take the streetcar, which incidentally follows the very same route? The reason: he refuses to take the streetcar because "he had no desire to humble himself before the committee of inquiry by a too-scrupulous punctuality." He runs to the tribunal, but he runs as a proud man who will not be humiliated.

Stage 2: Proof of strength. Finally, he arrives in the room where he is expected. "So you are a house painter?" says the examining magistrate, and K., in front of the crowd filling the hall, reacts spiritedly to the ridiculous mistake: "No, I'm the chief clerk of a large bank," and then, in a long speech, he lambastes the tribunal for its incompetence. Heartened by applause, he feels strong, and in the familiar cliché of the accused turned accuser (wonderfully deaf to Kafkan irony, Orson Welles was taken in by the cliché), he challenges his judges. The first shock comes when he notices badges on the collars of everyone there and realizes that the audience he thought to win over consists of officials "here to listen and snoop." He turns to leave, and at the door, the examining magistrate is waiting to warn him: "You have flung away with your own hand the advantage an interrogation always offers an accused man." K. exclaims: "You scum! You can keep all your interrogations!"

A reader will understand nothing about this scene unless he sees its ironic connections with what comes immediately after the rebellious outburst from K. that ends the chapter. Here is the start of the next chapter: "During the next week, day after day K. awaited a new summons; he could not believe that his refusal to be interrogated had been taken literally, and having heard nothing by Saturday evening, he assumed that he was tacitly required again in the same building and at the same time. So he again made his way there on Sunday. . . ."

Stage 3: Socialization of the trial. Alarmed by the case being brought against his nephew, K.'s uncle arrives one day from the country. A remarkable fact: the case, it's said, is utterly secret, confidential, yet everyone knows about it. Another remarkable fact: no one doubts that K. is guilty. Society has already adopted the accusation and added the weight of its tacit approval (or its nondisagreement). We would expect indignant surprise: "How could they accuse you? And for what crime, exactly?" But the uncle is not surprised. He is only frightened by the thought of the trial's consequences for all the relatives.

Stage 4: Self-criticism. In order to defend himself in a trial that refuses to declare the charge, K. ends up looking for the crime himself. Where is it concealed? Certainly somewhere in his curriculum vitae. "He would have to recall his entire life, including the most minute acts and events, and then to explain and examine it in every regard."

The situation is not at all unreal: this is actually the way some simple woman hounded by misfortune will wonder: what have I done wrong? and begin to

comb her past, examining not only her actions but her
words and her secret thoughts in an effort to comprehend God's anger.

To describe this state of mind, Communist political
practice coined the term *self-criticism* (used in this
political sense since the 1930s; Kafka never used it).
This usage of the term does not correspond exactly to
its etymology. It is not a matter of *criticism* (distin-
guishing good features from bad with the aim of correcting faults); it is a matter of *finding your offense* to
let you help your accuser, let you accept and ratify the
accusation.

*Stage 5: The victim's identification with his execu-
tioner.* Kafka's irony attains its horrifying peak in the
last chapter: two men in frock coats come for K. and
take him into the street. At first he struggles, but then
he thinks: "All I can do now . . . is keep a clear head to
the end. . . . Should I show now that I've learned nothing in a year of this trial? Should I go off like a dimwit
with no sense?"

Then, from a distance, he sees some policemen
walking their beats. One of them approaches this sus-
picious-looking group. Thereupon, on his own initiative, K. forcibly drags the two men away, even starting
to run with them to escape the policemen who, after
all, might disrupt or perhaps—who knows?—prevent
his coming execution.

Finally, they arrive at their destination; as the
men prepare to stab him, an idea (his ultimate self-
criticism) crosses K.'s mind: "It would be his duty to
seize the knife himself . . . and plunge it into his own
body." He deplores his weakness: "He could not prove
himself completely, he could not relieve the officials

of the whole task; the responsibility for this ultimate failing lay with the one who had denied him the remnant of strength he needed."

For How Long Can a Man Be Considered Identical to Himself?

In Dostoyevsky, the characters' identities lie in their personal ideology, which more or less directly determines their behavior. Kirilov, in *The Possessed,* is completely absorbed by his philosophy of suicide, which he considers to be a supreme manifestation of freedom. Kirilov: an idea become man. But in real life, is a man really such a direct projection of his personal ideology? Tolstoy's characters in *War and Peace* (particularly Pierre Bezukhov and Andrei Bolkonsky) also have a very rich, very developed intellectuality, but theirs is changeable, protean, so that it is impossible to describe them in terms of their ideas, which are different in each phase of their lives. Tolstoy thus offers us another conception of man: he is an itinerary; a winding road; a journey whose successive phases not only vary but often represent a total negation of the preceding phases.

I've said *road,* a word that could mislead, because the image of a road evokes a destination. Now, what is the destination of these roads that end only randomly, broken off by the happenstance of death? It's true that, at the end, Pierre Bezukhov arrives at the state of mind that seems to be the ideal and final stage: he comes to believe that it is futile to keep searching for a meaning to his life, to struggle for this or that cause;

God is everywhere, in all of life, in ordinary life, so it is enough to live all there is to live and live it lovingly: and he turns happily to his wife and family. Is his destination reached? The summit that, retrospectively, makes all the earlier stages of the journey into mere steps on the stairway? If that were the case, Tolstoy's novel would lose its essential irony and come to resemble a novelized morality lesson. But it is not the case. In the Epilogue that summarizes the events of the next eight years, we see Bezukhov leaving his house and wife for a month and a half to engage in some semi-clandestine political activity in Petersburg. So again he is off to seek a meaning to his life, to struggle for a cause. The roads never end and know no destinations.

One might say that the various phases of an itinerary do have an ironic relation to one another. In the kingdom of irony, equality rules; this means that no phase of the itinerary is morally superior to another. When Bolkonsky sets about the task of serving his country, is he seeking thereby *to expiate the wrong* of his earlier misanthropy? No. There is no self-criticism here. At each phase of the way, he focused all his intellectual and moral powers to arrive at his position, and he knows that; so how can he blame himself for not having been what he could not be? And just as one cannot pass judgment on the various phases of one's life from a moral viewpoint, similarly one cannot judge them as to authenticity. It is impossible to say which Bolkonsky is more true to himself: the one who withdrew from public life or the one who devoted himself to it.

If the various stages are so contradictory, how do we determine their common denominator? What is the common essence that lets us see Bezukhov the atheist and Bezukhov the believer as the selfsame person? Where does the stable essence of an "I" reside? And what moral responsibility does Bolkonsky No. 2 have toward Bolkonsky No. 1? Must the Bezukhov who is Napoleon's enemy answer for the Bezukhov who was once his admirer? Over what period of time can we consider a man identical to himself?

Only the novel can, in concrete terms, explore this mystery, one of the greatest known to man; and Tolstoy was probably the first to do so.

Conspiracy of Details

The metamorphoses of Tolstoy's characters come about not as a lengthy evolution but as a sudden illumination. Pierre Bezukhov is transformed from an atheist into a believer with astonishing ease. All it takes is for him to be shaken up by the break with his wife and to encounter at a post house a traveling Freemason who talks to him. That ease is not due to lightweight capriciousness. Rather, it shows us that the visible change was prepared by a hidden, unconscious process, which suddenly bursts into broad daylight.

Gravely wounded on the battlefield of Austerlitz, Andrei Bolkonsky is regaining consciousness. At this moment his entire universe, that of a brilliant young man, is set rocking: not by rational, logical reflection, but by a direct confrontation with death and a long look at the sky. It is such details (a look at the sky) that play a great role in the decisive moments experienced by Tolstoy's characters.

Later on, emerging from his deep skepticism, Andrei returns to an active life. This change is preceded by a long discussion with Pierre on a ferry crossing a river. Pierre at the time is positive, optimistic, altruistic (such is that brief stage in his evolution), and he disputes Andrei's misanthropic skepticism. But in their discussion he shows himself rather naïve, spouting clichés, and it is Andrei who shines intellectually. More important than Pierre's words is the silence that follows their discussion: "Stepping off the ferry he looked up at the sky to which Pierre had pointed. For the first time since Austerlitz he saw that high everlasting sky he had seen while lying on the battlefield, and something that had long been slumbering, something better that was within him, suddenly awoke, joyful and youthful, in his soul." The sensation is short-lived and vanishes immediately, but Andrei knows "that this feeling, *which he did not know how to develop, was alive in him*." And one day much later, like a dance of sparks, a *conspiracy of details* (the sight of an oak tree's foliage, the happy talk of girls overheard by chance, unexpected memories) kindles that feeling (that "was alive in him") and sets it blazing. Andrei, still content the day before in his retreat from the world, abruptly decides "to go to Petersburg that autumn" and even "re-enter government service. . . . And Prince Andrei, clasping his hands behind his back, paced back and forth in the room for a long time, now frowning, now smiling, as he reflected on *all those irrational, inexpressible thoughts, secret as a crime, that were connected with Pierre, with fame, with the girl at the window, with the oak, with woman's beauty and with love*, which had altered his whole life. And if anyone came into the room at such moments he was particularly curt, stern, firm, and, above all, disagreeably logical . . . as if to punish someone for all *the secret, illogical work going on within him.*" (I emphasize the most significant lines.) (Let us recall that it is a similar conspiracy of details— the ugliness of faces around her, conversation overheard by chance in the train compartment, intractable memories—that, in Tolstoy's next novel, touches off Anna Karenina's decision to kill herself.)

Still another great change in Andrei Bolkonsky's internal world: mortally wounded in the battle of Borodino, he lies on an operating table in a military encampment and is suddenly filled with a strange sense of peace and reconciliation, a sense of happiness, which will stay with him; this state of happiness is all the stranger (and all the more beautiful) for the enormous harshness of the scene, which is full of the hideously precise details of surgery in a time before anesthesia; and strangest of all about this strange state: it is provoked by an unexpected and illogical memory: when the doctor's assistant removed his clothes, "Andrei recalled his earliest, most remote childhood." And some lines farther on: "After the agony he had been enduring, Prince Andrei enjoyed a blissful feeling such as he had not experienced for a long time. All the best and happiest moments of his life, especially those of early childhood—when he had been undressed and put to bed, and when his nurse had sung him lullabies and he had buried his head in the pillow and felt happy just to be alive—rose to his mind, not as something past, but as a present reality." Only later does Andrei recognize, on a nearby operating table, his rival, Anatol, Natasha's seducer, whose leg has just been cut off by a doctor.

The usual reading of this scene: Wounded, Andrei sees his rival with his leg amputated; the sight fills him with immense pity for the man and for man in general. But Tolstoy knew that these sudden revelations are not due to causes so obvious and so logical. It was a curious fleeting image (the early-childhood memory of being undressed in the same way as the doctor's assistant was doing it) that touched everything off—his new metamorphosis, his new vision of things. A few seconds later, this miraculous detail has certainly been forgotten by Andrei himself just as it has probably been immediately forgotten by the majority of readers, who read novels as inattentively and badly as they "read" their own lives.

And another great change, this time Pierre Bezukhov's decision to kill Napoleon, a decision preceded by this episode: He learns from his Freemason friends that in Chapter 13 of the Apocalypse, Napoleon is identified as the Antichrist: "Let him that hath understanding count the number of the beast: for it is the number of a man; and his number is Six hundred threescore and six." When the French alphabet is given numerical values, the letters in *"l'empereur Napoléon"* add up to the number 666.

"This prophecy greatly surprised Pierre, and he often asked himself what exactly would put an end to the power of the beast, that is, of Napoleon, and tried, by the same system of turning letters into numbers and adding them up, to find an answer to the question that engrossed him. He wrote the words *l'empereur Alexandre* and *la nation russe* and added up their numbers. But the sums were either more or less than 666. Once when making such calculations he wrote down his own name in French, *comte Pierre Bésouhoff*; the sum was far from right. He changed the spelling, substituting a *z* for the *s* and adding *de* and the article *le*, still without obtaining the desired result. Then it occurred to him that if the answer to the question were contained in his name, his nationality would also be given in the answer. So he wrote *le Russe Bésuhof*, and adding up the numbers got 671. This was only five too much; five was represented by *e*, the very letter elided from the article *le* before the word *empereur*. By omitting the *e*, though incorrectly, Pierre got the answer he sought: *l'Russe Bésuhof* made 666. This discovery greatly excited him."

Tolstoy's meticulousness in describing all the spelling changes Pierre works on his own name so as to get to the number 666 is irresistibly comic: *l'Russe* is a marvelous orthographic gag. Can grave and courageous decisions of an unquestionably intelligent and likable man be rooted in some foolish idea?

And what are your thoughts on man? What are your thoughts on yourself?

Change of Opinion as Adjustment to the Spirit of the Time

One day, with a radiant face, a woman declares to me: "So, there's no more Leningrad! We're back to good old Saint Petersburg!" It never did thrill me, cities and streets being rechristened. I am about to tell her this, but at the last moment I control myself: in her gaze, bedazzled by the fascinating march of history, I foresee disagreement, and I have no desire to argue, especially because just then I recall an episode she has certainly forgotten. This same woman came from abroad to visit my wife and me in Prague after the Russian invasion, in 1970 or 1971, when we were in the painful situation of being under ban. She was showing her solidarity with us, and we wanted to pay her back by trying to entertain her. My wife told her the funny story (it was oddly prophetic besides) of an American moneybags staying in a Moscow hotel. Someone asks him: "Have you been to see Lenin in the mausoleum?" And he replies: "For ten dollars I had him brought over to the hotel." Our visitor's face tensed. A leftist (she still is), she saw the Russian invasion of Czechoslovakia as a betrayal of ideals she cherished, and felt it unacceptable that victims with whom she meant to sympathize should mock those same betrayed ideals. "I don't find that funny," she said coldly, and only our status as persecuted people saved us from a break with her.

I can tell lots of stories of this kind. Such changes of opinion involve not only politics but also attitudes generally—admiration followed by scorn for the "*nouveau roman*," revolutionary puritanism supplanted by libertarian pornography, the idea of Europe denigrated as reactionary and neocolonialist by people who later unfurled it as a banner of Progress, and so on. And I wonder: do they or do they not recall their earlier attitudes? Do they retain any memory of the history of their changes? Not that it angers me to see people change their opinions. Bezukhov, formerly an admirer of Napoleon, becomes his potential assassin, and I like him just as much in the one role as in the other.

Doesn't a woman who worshiped Lenin in 1971 have the right to rejoice in 1991 that Leningrad is no longer Leningrad? She certainly does. Her change, however, is different from Bezukhov's.

It is precisely when their interior worlds change shape that Bezukhov and Bolkonsky are confirmed as individuals; that they surprise; that they make themselves different; that their freedom catches fire, and with it the identity of their selves; these are moments of poetry: they experience them with such intensity that the whole world rushes forward to meet them with an intoxicating parade of wondrous details. In Tolstoy, man is the more himself, the more an individual, when he has the strength, the imagination, the intelligence, to transform himself.

By contrast, the people I see changing their attitude toward Lenin, Europe, and so on expose their nonindividuality. This change is neither their own creation nor their own invention, not caprice or surprise or thought or madness; it has no poetry; it is nothing but a very prosaic adjustment to the changing spirit of History. That is why they don't even notice it; in the final analysis, they always stay the same: always in the right, always thinking what, in their milieu, a person is supposed to think; they change not in order to draw closer to some essential self but in order to merge with everyone else; changing lets them stay unchanged.

Another way of expressing it: they change their mind in accordance with the invisible tribunal that is also changing its mind; their change is thus simply a bet on what the tribunal will proclaim to be the truth tomorrow. I remember my youth in Czechoslovakia. Having emerged from our initial enchantment with

Communism, we felt each small step against official doctrine to be a courageous act. We protested the persecution of religious believers, stood up for banned modern art, argued against the stupidity of propaganda, criticized the country's dependence on Russia, and so on. In doing so, we were taking some risk—not much, but still some—and that (little) danger gave us a pleasant moral satisfaction. One day a hideous thought came to me: what if our rebellions were dictated not by internal freedom, by courage, but by the desire to please the other tribunal that was already preparing, in the shadows, to sit in judgment?

Windows

No one can go further than Kafka in *The Trial*; he created the extremely poetic image of an extremely nonpoetic world. By "extremely nonpoetic world" I mean: a world where there is no longer a place for individual freedom, for the uniqueness of the individual, where man is only the instrument of extrahuman forces: of bureaucracy, technology, History. By "extremely poetic image" I mean: without changing its essence and its nonpoetic nature, Kafka has transformed, reshaped that world by his immense poetic imagination.

K. is completely absorbed by the predicament of this trial that has been imposed upon him; he hasn't a moment to think about anything else. And yet, even in this no-way-out predicament, there are windows that open suddenly, for a brief instant. He cannot escape through these windows; they edge open and then shut instantly; but for a flash at least, he can see the poetry

of the world outside, the poetry that, despite everything, exists as an ever present possibility and sends a
small silvery glint into his life as a hunted man.

Some such brief openings are K.'s glances, for
instance: he reaches the suburban street where he has
been called for his first interrogation. A moment
before, he was still running to get there on time. Now
he stops. Standing in the street, he forgets the trial for
a few seconds and looks around: "Most of the windows
were occupied, men in shirtsleeves were leaning there
smoking or holding little children carefully and ten-
derly on the windowsills. Other windows were piled
high with bedding, above which the disheveled head of
a woman would appear for a moment." Then he enters
the courtyard: "Near him a barefooted man was sitting
on a crate reading a newspaper. Two boys were see-
sawing on a handcart. A frail young girl was standing
at a pump in her nightdress and gazing at K. while she
filled her jug with water."

These sentences remind me of Flaubert's descriptions: concise; visually rich; a sense of detail, none of
which is clichéd. That power of description makes
clear how thirsty K. is for reality, how avidly he drinks
up the world that, just a moment earlier, was eclipsed
by worries about the trial. Alas, the pause is short; the
next instant K. no longer has eyes for the frail young
girl in her nightdress filling her jug with water: the tor-
rent of the trial takes him up again.

The few erotic situations in the novel are also like
windows briefly ajar—very briefly: K. meets only
women who are connected in one way or another to his
trial: for instance, his neighbor Fräulein Bürstner, in
whose room he had been arrested; troubled, K. tells

her what happened and finally, at her door, he manages to kiss her: "He seized her and kissed her on the mouth, and then all over the face, like some *thirsty* animal lapping greedily at a long-sought spring." I emphasize the word "thirsty," which gives the sense of a man who has lost his normal life and can contact it only furtively, through a window.

During the first interrogation, K. is making a speech but is thrown off track by a curious event: the bailiff's wife is in the room, and a scrawny, ugly student gets her down on the floor and is making love to her in the midst of the audience. With this amazing interplay of incompatible events (that sublime Kafkan poetry, grotesque and implausible!), a new window opens onto the landscape far from the trial, onto exuberant vulgarity, the exuberant vulgar freedom that has been confiscated from K.

That Kafkan poetry reminds me, by contrast, of another novel that is also about an arrest and a trial: Orwell's *1984*, the book that for decades served as a constant reference for antitotalitarianism professionals. In this novel, which means to be the horrifying portrayal of an imaginary totalitarian society, there are no windows; in it no one glimpses a frail young girl filling a jug with water; Orwell's novel is firmly closed to poetry; did I say novel? it is political thought disguised as a novel; the thinking is certainly lucid and correct, but it is distorted by its guise as a novel, which renders it imprecise and vague. So if the novel form obscures Orwell's thought, does it give something in return? Does it throw light on the mystery of human situations that sociology or political science cannot get at? No: the situations and the characters are as flat as a poster.

Then is it justified at least as a popularization of good ideas? Not that either. For ideas made into a novel function no longer as ideas but as a novel instead— and in the case of *1984*, as a *bad* novel, with all the pernicious influence a bad novel can exert.

The pernicious influence of Orwell's novel resides in its implacable reduction of a reality to its political dimension alone, and in its reduction of that dimension to what is exemplarily negative about it. I refuse to forgive this reduction on the grounds that it was useful as propaganda in the struggle against totalitarian evil. For that evil is, precisely, the reduction of life to politics and of politics to propaganda. So despite its intentions, Orwell's novel itself joins in the totalitarian spirit, the spirit of propaganda. It reduces (and teaches others to reduce) the life of a hated society to the simple listing of its crimes.

In talking with Czechs a year or two after the end of Communism, I would hear from every one of them that now-ritual turn of speech, that obligatory preamble to all their recollections, all their remarks: "after those forty years of Communist horror" or: "those horrible forty years" or especially: "the forty lost years." I looked at my interlocutors: they had been neither forced to emigrate, nor imprisoned, nor deprived of their jobs, nor even looked down on; all of them had lived their lives in their own country, in their apartments, had done their work and had their vacations, their friendships and their loves; with the expression "forty horrible years" they were reducing their lives to the political aspect alone. But even the political history of those forty years—did they really experience that only as an undifferentiated block of horrors? Have they forgotten the years when they were seeing Milos Forman's films, reading Bohuslav Hrabal's books, going to the little nonconformist theaters, and telling hundreds of jokes and cheerfully making fun of the regime? In their talk of forty horrible years, they were all *Orwellizing* the recollection of their own lives, which, a posteriori, in their memories and in their heads, were thereby devalued or even completely obliterated (forty *lost* years).

Even in his situation of extreme deprivation of freedom, K. is able to look at a frail young girl slowly filling her jug with water. I've said that such moments are windows that briefly open onto a landscape far away from K.'s trial. What landscape? To develop the metaphor: the windows in Kafka's novel open onto Tolstoy's landscape: onto a world where, even at the harshest moments, characters retain a freedom of decision which gives life the happy incalculability that is the source of poetry. The extremely poetic world of Tolstoy is the opposite of Kafka's world. But even so, because of the half-open window, it enters K.'s story like a breath of yearning, like a barely felt breeze, and stays there.

Tribunal and Trial

The philosophers of existence like to breathe philosophical significance into the words of everyday language. It is difficult for me to say the words *anguish* or *talk* without thinking of the meaning Heidegger gave them. On this score, the novelists preceded the philosophers. In examining their characters' situations, they worked out their own vocabulary, often with key words that stand as concepts and go beyond the dictionary definitions. Thus Crébillon the younger used the word *moment* as a concept word for the libertine game (the moment of opportunity when a woman can be seduced) and bequeathed it to his time and to other writers. In the same way, Dostoyevsky spoke of *humiliation* and Stendhal of *vanity*. Thanks to *The Trial*, Kafka bequeathed to us at least two concept words that have become indispensable for understanding the modern world: *tribunal* and *trial*. He bequeathed them to us: meaning that he put them at our disposal, for us to use, consider, and reconsider in terms of our own experiences.

Tribunal: this does not signify the juridical institution intended for punishing people who have violated the laws of a state; the tribunal (or court) in Kafka's sense is a power that judges, that judges because it is a power; its power and nothing but its power is what confers legitimacy on the tribunal; when the two intruders enter his room, K. immediately recognizes that power, and he submits.

The trial brought by the tribunal is always *absolute*; meaning that it does not concern an isolated act, a specific crime (theft, fraud, rape), but rather concerns the character of the accused in its entirety: K. searches for his offense in "the most minute events" of his *whole* life; in our century, by this standard, Bezukhov would have been indicted for both his love and his hatred of Napoleon. And also for his drunkennness, since, being absolute, the trial concerns private life as well as public; Brod condemned K. to death for seeing in women only the "lowest sexuality"; I recall the 1951 political trials in Prague; biographies of the accused were distributed in enormous printings; that was the first time I read a piece of pornography: the account of an orgy during which the naked body of a female defendant was coated with chocolate (at that peak of shortages!) and licked by the tongues of other defendants, soon to be hanged; at the start of the gradual collapse of the Communist ideology, the trial of Karl Marx (a trial that has lately culminated in the razing of his statues in Russia and elsewhere) opened with an attack on his private life (the first anti-Marx book I ever read: the account of his sexual relations with his housemaid); in *The Joke*, three other students are trying Ludvik over a sentence he has written his girlfriend; defending himself, he says he dashed it off in haste, without thinking; they answer: "you could only have written what was *inside* you"; because everything the defendant says, murmurs, thinks, everything he has hidden inside him is to be put at the tribunal's disposal.

The trial is absolute as well in that it does not keep within the limits of the defendant's life; thus K.'s uncle says: "Do you want to lose this trial? . . . It means that you will be absolutely ruined. And all your relatives along with you." The guilt of one Jew contains within it that of the Jews of all times; the Communist doctrine on the influence of class origin includes within the offense of the accused the offense of his parents and grandparents; in the trial of Europe for the crime of colonialism, Sartre accused not the colonists but Europe, *all* of Europe, the Europe of *all times*; because "there is a colonist in each of us," because "being a man here means being an accomplice since we have *all* profited from colonial exploitation." The spirit of the trial recognizes no statute of limitations; the distant past is as alive as today's event; and even in death you will not escape: there are informers in the cemetery.

The trial's memory is colossal, but it is a very specific memory, which could be defined as *the forgetting of everything not a crime*. The trial thus reduces the defendant's biography to *criminography*; Victor Farias (whose *Heidegger and Nazism* is a classic example of criminography) locates the roots of the philosopher's Nazism in his early youth, without the least concern for locating the roots of his genius; to punish someone accused of ideological deviations, Communist tribunals would put *all* his work on the index (thus, for instance, the ban on Lukács and Sartre in Communist countries covered even their pro-Communist writings). "Why are our streets still named for Picasso, Aragon, Éluard, Sartre?" a Paris paper asked in a 1991 post-Communist intoxication; it's tempting to answer: because of the value of their works! But in his trial against Europe, Sartre said exactly what values mean now: "our cherished values are losing their wings; looked at closely, every one of them is blood-stained"; values stained are values no longer; the spirit of the trial is the reduction of everything to morality; it is absolute nihilism in regard to craft, art, works.

Even before the intruders come in to arrest him, K. sees the old woman in the house across the way gazing at him "with totally unusual curiosity"; thus, from the beginning, the *ancient chorus of concierges* enters the game; in *The Castle*, Amalia is neither accused nor convicted, but it is widely known that the invisible tribunal dislikes her, and that is enough to keep all the villagers away from her; because if the tribunal imposes a *trial-regime* on a country, the entire population is dragooned into the grand machinations of the trial, increasing its efficacy a hundredfold; every single person knows that he could be accused at any moment, and he ponders his self-criticism in advance; self-criticism: the subjection of the accused to the accuser; the renunciation of his self; a way of nullifying himself as an individual; after the Communist revolution of 1948, the daughter of a wealthy Czech family felt guilty about her undeserved privileges as a child of affluence; to show her repentance, she became so fervent a Communist that she publicly repudiated her father; now, after the disappearance of Communism, she is again undergoing judgment and again feeling guilty; ground between the millstones of two trials, of two self-criticisms, all she has behind her is the desert of a repudiated life; even though in the meantime all the houses once confiscated from her (repudiated) father have been returned to her, today she is merely a nullified creature; doubly nullified; self-nullified.

For a trial is initiated not to render justice but to annihilate the defendant; as Brod said: he who does not love anyone, who only dallies, must die; thus K. is stabbed in the heart; Bukharin is shot. Even when the trial is of dead people, the point is to kill them off a second time: by burning their books; by removing their names from the schoolbooks; by demolishing their monuments; by rechristening the streets that bore their names.

The Trial Against the Century

For nearly seventy years Europe lived under a trial-
regime. From among the great artists of the century,
how many defendants . . . I shall mention only those
who had some significance for me. Starting in the
twenties, there were those hounded by the tribunal of
revolutionary morality: Bunin, Andreyev, Meyerhold,
Pilnyak, Veprik (a Jewish-Russian musician, a forgotten martyr of modern art; he dared to defend
Shostakovich's opera against Stalin's condemnation;
they stuck him in a camp; I remember his piano compositions, which my father liked to play), Mandelstam,
Halas (the poet who was adored by Ludvik in *The
Joke*; hounded after his death for gloominess seen as
counterrevolutionary). Then there were the quarry of
the Nazi tribunal: Broch (he gazes at me, pipe in
mouth, from a photo on my worktable), Schoenberg,
Werfel, Brecht, Thomas and Heinrich Mann, Musil,
Vancura (the Czech writer I love most), Bruno Schulz.
The totalitarian empires and their bloody trials have
disappeared, but the *spirit of the trial* lingers as a
legacy, and that is what is now settling scores. Thus
the trial strikes at: those accused of pro-Nazi sympathies: Hamsun, Heidegger (all Czech dissident thought,
Patocka most notably, is indebted to him), Richard
Strauss, Gottfried Benn, von Doderer, Drieu la Rochelle,
Céline (in 1992, a half century after the war, an indignant official refused to designate his house a historical monument); supporters of Mussolini: Malaparte,
Marinetti, Pirandello, Ezra Pound (the American military kept him, like an animal, in a cage for months
under the blazing Italian sun; in his Reykjavik studio, the

painter Kristján Davidsson showed me a large photo of him: "For fifty years it has gone with me everywhere I go"); the Munich appeasers: Giono, Alain, Morand, Montherlant, St.-John Perse (a member of the French delegation to the Munich conference, he was closely involved in the humiliation of my native country); then, the Communists and their sympathizers: Mayakovsky (who today remembers his love poetry and his amazing metaphors?), Gorky, Shaw, Brecht (who is thereby undergoing his second trial), Éluard (that exterminating angel who used to decorate his signature with a drawing of crossed swords), Picasso, Léger, Aragon (how can I forget that he offered me his hand at a difficult time in my life?), Nezval (his self-portrait in oils is on the wall by my bookshelves), Sartre. Some of these people are undergoing a double trial, first accused of betraying the revolution, then accused for services they had rendered it earlier: Gide (in the old Communist countries, the symbol of all evil), Shostakovich (to atone for his difficult music, he manufactured rubbish for the regime's needs; he maintained that for the history of art a worthless thing is null and void; he didn't know that for the tribunal it is the worthlessness itself that counts), Breton, Malraux (accused yesterday of having betrayed revolutionary ideals, accusable tomorrow of having held them), Tibor Déry (some works of this Communist writer, who was imprisoned after the Budapest massacre, were for me the first great *literary*, nonpropagandistic reply to Stalinism). The most exquisite flower of the century, the modern art of the twenties and thirties, was even triply accused: first by the Nazi tribunal as *Entartete Kunst*, "degenerate art"; then by the Communist tri-

bunal as "elitist formalism alien to the people"; and
finally by the triumphant capitalist tribunal as art
steeped in revolutionary illusions.

How is it possible that the Soviet Russian chauvin-
ist, the maker of versified propaganda, he whom Stalin
himself called "the greatest poet of our epoch"—how is
it possible that Mayakovsky is nevertheless a tremendous poet, one of the greatest? Given her capacity for
enthusiasm, her emotional tears that blur her view of
the outside world, wasn't lyric poetry—that untouch-
able goddess—doomed one fateful day to become the
beautifier of atrocities, their "warmhearted maidser-
vant" (Baudelaire)? These are the questions that fascinated me when, some twenty-five years ago, I wrote
Life Is Elsewhere, the novel in which Jaromil, a poet
under twenty years old, becomes the elated servant of
the Stalinist regime. I was aghast when critics,
although praising my book, saw my hero as a fake
poet, a bastard even. In my view, Jaromil is an authentic poet, an innocent soul; otherwise, I would not have
seen any interest to my novel. Am I the one to blame
for the misunderstanding? Did I express myself badly?
I don't think so. To be a true poet and at the same time
to support (like Jaromil or Mayakovsky) an incon-
testable horror is a *scandal*—in the sense of an unjustifiable, unacceptable event, one that contradicts logic
and yet is real. We are all unconsciously tempted to
dodge scandals, to behave as though they don't exist.
That is why we prefer to say that the great cultural figures tainted with the horrors of our century were *bas-
tards*; that's logical, that's in the nature of things; but
it isn't so; if only out of vanity, aware that they are
seen, looked at, judged, artists and philosophers are

anxious to be decent and courageous, to be on the right side, to be right. That makes the scandal still more inexplicable. If we don't want to leave this century just as stupid as we entered it, we must abandon the facile moralism of the trial and think about the enigma of this scandal, think it through to the bottom, even if this should lead us to question anew all our certainties about man as such.

But the conformism of public opinion is a force that sets itself up as a tribunal, and the tribunal is not there to waste time over ideas, it is there to conduct the investigations for trials. And as the abyss of time widens between judges and defendants, it is always a lesser experience that is judging a greater. The immature sit in judgment on Céline's erring ways without realizing that because of these erring ways, Céline's novels contain existential knowledge that, if they were to understand it, could make them more adult. Because therein lies the power of culture: it redeems horror by transforming it into existential wisdom. If the spirit of the trial succeeds in annihilating this century's culture, nothing will remain of us but a memory of its atrocities sung by a chorus of children.

Those with No Sense of Guilt Are Dancing

The music (commonly and vaguely) called "rock " has been inundating the sonic environment of daily life for twenty years; it seized possession of the world at the very moment when the twentieth century was disgust-

232

edly vomiting up its history; a question haunts me: was this coincidence mere chance? Or is there some hidden meaning to the conjunction of the century's final trials and the ecstasy of rock? Is the century hoping to forget itself in this ecstatic howling? To forget its utopias foundering in horror? To forget its art? An art whose subtlety, whose needless complexity, irritates the populace, offends against democracy?

The word "rock" is vague; therefore, I would rather describe the music I mean: human voices prevail over instruments, high-pitched voices over low ones; there is no contrast to the dynamics, which keep to a perpetual fortissimo that turns the singing into howling; as in jazz, the rhythm accentuates the second beat of the measure, but in a more stereotyped and noisier manner; the harmony and the melody are simplistic and thus they bring out the tone color, the only inventive element of this music; while the popular songs of the first half of the century had melodies that made poor folk cry (and delighted Mahler's and Stravinsky's musical irony), this so-called rock music is exempt from the sin of sentimentality; it is not sentimental, it is ecstatic, it is the prolongation of a single moment of ecstasy; and since ecstasy is a moment wrenched out of time—a brief moment without memory, a moment surrounded by forgetting—the melodic motif has no room to develop, it only repeats, without evolving or concluding (rock is the only "light" music in which melody is not predominant; people don't hum rock melodies).

A curious thing: thanks to the technology of sound reproduction, this ecstatic music resounds incessantly and everywhere, and thus outside ecstatic situations.

The acoustic image of ecstasy has become the everyday decor of our lassitude. It is inviting us to no orgy, to no mystical experience, so what does this trivialized ecstasy mean to tell us? That we should accept it. That we should get used to it. That we should respect its privileged position. That we should observe the *ethic* it decrees.

The ethic of ecstasy is the opposite of the trial's ethic; under its protection everybody does whatever he wants: now anyone can suck his thumb as he likes, from infancy to graduation, and it is a freedom no one will be willing to give up; look around you on the Métro; seated or standing, every single person has a finger in some orifice of his face—in the ear, in the mouth, in the nose; no one feels he's being observed, and everyone dreams of writing a book to tell about his unique and inimitable self, which is picking its nose; no one listens to anyone else, everyone writes, and each of them writes the way rock is danced to: alone, for himself, focused on himself yet making the same motions as all the others. In this situation of *uniform egocentricity*, the sense of guilt does not play the role it once did; the tribunals still operate, but they are fascinated exclusively by the past; they see only the core of the century; they see only the generations that are old or dead. Kafka's characters were made to feel guilty by the authority of the father; it is because his father disgraces him that the hero of "The Judgment" drowns himself in a river; that time is past: in the world of rock, the father has been charged with such a load of guilt that, for a long time now, he allows everything. Those with no guilt feelings are dancing.

Recently, two adolescents murdered a priest: on

television I heard another priest talking, his voice trembling with understanding: "We must pray for the priest who was a victim of his mission: he was especially concerned with young people. But we must also pray for the two unfortunate adolescents; they too were victims: of their drives."

While freedom of thought—freedom of words, of attitudes, of jokes, of reflection, of dangerous ideas, of intellectual provocations—shrinks, under surveillance as it is by the vigilance of the tribunal of general conformism, *the freedom of drives* grows ever greater. They are preaching severity against sins of thought; they are preaching forgiveness for crimes committed in emotional ecstasy.

Paths in the Fog

Robert Musil's contemporaries admired his intelligence much more than his books; they said he should have written essays, not novels. A negative proof suffices to refute this opinion: read Musil's essays: how heavy they are, boring and charmless! For Musil is a great thinker *only* in his novels. His thought needs to feed on concrete situations and concrete characters; in short, it is *novelistic thought*, not philosophic.

Each first chapter of the eighteen books of Fielding's *Tom Jones* is a brief essay. Its first French translator, in the eighteenth century, purely and simply eliminated all of them, claiming that they were not to the French taste. Turgenev reproached Tolstoy for the essayistic passages in *War and Peace* dealing with the philosophy of history. Tolstoy began to doubt himself and, under pressure of advisers, eliminated those passages in the third edition of the novel. Fortunately, he later restored them.

Just as there are novelistic dialogue and action, there is also novelistic reflection. The lengthy historical reflections in *War and Peace* are inconceivable outside of the novel—for instance, in a scholarly journal. Because of their language, certainly, which is filled with intentionally naïve similes and metaphors. But above all because Tolstoy talking about history is not interested, as a historian would be, in the exact account of events and of their consequences for social, political, and cultural life, in the evaluation of this or that person's role, and so on; he is interested in history as a *new dimension of human existence*.

History became a concrete experience for everyone toward the start of the nineteenth century, during the Napoleonic Wars that figure in *War and Peace*; with a shock, these wars made clear to every European that the world around him was subject to perpetual change that interferes with his life, transforming it and keeping it in motion. Before the nineteenth century, wars and rebellions were felt to be natural catastrophes, like the plague or an earthquake. People saw neither unity nor continuity in historical events, and did not believe it possible to influence their course. Diderot's Jacques the Fatalist joins a regiment and then is seriously wounded in battle; marked for life, he will limp for the rest of his days. But what battle was it? The novel doesn't say. And why should it say? All wars were the same. In eighteenth-century novels the historical moment is specified only very approximately. Only after the start of the nineteenth century, from

Scott and Balzac on, do all wars no longer seem the same and characters in novels live in precisely dated times.

Tolstoy looks back on the Napoleonic Wars from a distance of fifty years. In his case, the new perception of history not only affects the structure of the novel, which has become more and more capable of capturing (in dialogue, in description) the historical nature of narrated events; but what interests him primarily is man's relation to history (his ability to dominate it or to escape it, to be free or not in regard to it), and he takes up the problem directly, as the very *theme* of his novel, a theme he explores by every means, including novelistic reflection.

Tolstoy argues against the idea that history is made by the will and reason of great individuals. History makes itself, he says, obeying laws of its own, which remain obscure to man. Great individuals "all were the *involuntary tools* of history, carrying on a work that was *concealed from them*." Later on: "Providence compelled all these men, each striving to attain personal aims, to combine in the accomplishment of a single stupendous result not one of them (neither Napoleon nor Alexander and still less anyone who did the actual fighting) *in the least expected*." And again: "Man lives consciously for himself, but is *unconsciously* a tool in the attainment of the historic, general aims of mankind." From which comes this tremendous conclusion: "*History, that is, the unconscious, general herd-life of mankind . . .* " (I emphasize the key phrases.)

With this conception of history, Tolstoy lays out the metaphysical space in which his characters move. Knowing neither the meaning nor the future course of history, knowing not even the objective meaning of their own actions (by which they "involuntarily" participate in events whose meaning is "concealed from them"), they proceed through their lives as one proceeds *in the fog*. I say fog, not darkness. In the darkness, we see nothing, we are blind, we are defenseless, we are not free. In the fog, we are free, but it is the freedom of a person in fog: he sees fifty yards ahead of him, he can clearly make out the features of his interlocutor, can take pleasure in the beauty of the trees that line the path, and can even observe what is happening close by and react.

Man proceeds in the fog. But when he looks back to judge people of the past, he sees no fog on their path. From his present, which was their faraway future, their path looks perfectly clear to him, good visibility all the way. Looking back, he sees the path, he sees the people proceeding, he sees their mistakes, but not the fog. And yet all of them—Heidegger, Mayakovsky, Aragon, Ezra Pound, Gorky, Gottfried Benn, St.-John Perse, Giono—all were walking in fog, and one might wonder: who is more blind? Mayakovsky, who as he wrote his poem on Lenin did not know where Leninism would lead? Or we, who judge him decades later and do not see the fog that enveloped him?

Mayakovsky's blindness is part of the eternal human condition.

But for us not to see the fog on Mayakovsky's path is to forget what man is, forget what we ourselves are.

PART NINE

You're Not in Your Own House Here, My Dear Fellow

1

Toward the end of his life, Stravinsky decided to bring his whole oeuvre together in a great recorded edition of his own performances, as pianist or conductor, so as to establish an authorized sonic version of all his music. This wish to take on the role of performer himself often provoked an irritated response: how fiercely Ernest Ansermet mocked him in his 1961 book: when Stravinsky conducts an orchestra, he is seized "by such panic that, for fear of falling, he pushes his music stand up against the podium rail, cannot take his eyes off a score he knows by heart, and counts time!"; he interprets his own music "literally and slavishly"; "when he performs all joy deserts him."

Why such sarcasm?

I open the Stravinsky letters: the correspondence with Ansermet starts in 1914; 146 letters by Stravinsky: My dear Ansermet, My dear fellow, My dear friend,

Very dear, My dear Ernest; not a hint of tension; then, like a thunderclap:

"Paris, October 14, 1937:

"In great haste, my dear fellow.

"There is absolutely no reason to make cuts in *Jeu de cartes* in concert performances. . . . Compositions of this type are dance suites whose form is rigorously symphonic and require no audience explanation, because there are no descriptive elements illustrating theatrical action, which would interfere with the symphonic evolution of the pieces as they are played in sequence.

"If this strange idea occurred to you, of asking me to make cuts, it must be that you personally find the sequence of movements in *Jeu de cartes* a little boring. I cannot do anything about that. But what amazes me most is that you try to convince *me* to make cuts in it—me, who just conducted it in Venice and who reported to you the enthusiastic response of the audience. Either you forgot what I told you, or else you do not attach much importance to my observations or to my critical sense. Furthermore, I really do not believe that your audience would be less intelligent than the one in Venice.

"And to think that it is you who proposed to cut my composition, with every likelihood of distorting it, in order that it might be better understood by the public—you, who were not afraid to play a work as risky from the standpoint of success and listener comprehension as the *Symphonies of Wind Instruments*!

"So I cannot let you make cuts in *Jeu de cartes*; I think it is better not to play it at all than to do so with reservations.

"I have nothing to add, period."

On October 15, Ansermet's reply:

"I ask only if you would forgive me the small cut in the March from the second measure after 45 to the second measure after 58."

Stravinsky reacted on October 19:

". . . I am sorry, but I cannot allow you *any* cuts in *Jeu de cartes*.

"The absurd one that you propose *cripples* my little March, which has its form and its structural meaning in the totality of the composition (a *structural meaning* that you claim to be protecting). You cut my March only because you like the middle section and the development less than the rest. In my view, this is not sufficient reason, and I would like to say: 'But you're not in your own house, my dear fellow'; I never told you: 'Here, take my score and do whatever you please with it.'

"I repeat: either you play *Jeu de cartes* as it is or you do not play it at all.

"You do not seem to have understood that my letter of October 14 was quite categorical on this point."

Thereafter they exchanged only a few letters, chilly, laconic. In 1961 Ansermet published in Switzerland a voluminous book of musicology, including a lengthy chapter that is an attack on the insensitivity of Stravinsky's music (and his incompetence as a conductor). Only in 1966 (twenty-nine years after their dispute) was there this brief response from Stravinsky to a conciliatory letter from Ansermet:

"My dear Ansermet,

"Your letter touched me. We are both too old not to think about the end of our days; and I would not want to end these days with the painful burden of an enmity."

An archetypal phrase for an archetypal situation:

often toward the end of their lives, friends who have
failed one another will call off their hostility this way,
coldly, without quite becoming friends again.

It's clear what was at stake in the dispute that
wrecked the friendship: Stravinsky's author's rights, his
moral rights; the anger of an author who will not stand
for anyone tampering with his work; and, on the other
side, the annoyance of a performer who cannot tolerate
the author's proud behavior and tries to limit his power.

2

As I listen to Leonard Bernstein's recording of *Le Sacre
du printemps*, something seems odd about the famous
lyrical passage for E-flat clarinet in the "*Rondes print-
anières*"; I turn to the score:

In Bernstein's performance, this becomes:

The novel charm of the passage above lies in the tension between the melodic lyricism and the rhythm, which is both mechanical and weirdly irregular; if this rhythm is not executed exactly, with clockwork precision, if it is *rubatoed*, if the last note of each phrase is stretched out (which Bernstein does), the tension disappears and the passage becomes commonplace.

I think of Ansermet's sarcasms. I prefer Stravinsky's performance, a hundred times over, even if he does push "his music stand up against the podium rail . . . and counts time."

3

In his book on Janacek, Jaroslav Vogel, himself a conductor, discusses Kovarovic's alterations to the score of *Jenufa*. He approves them and defends them. An astonishing attitude, for even if Kovarovic's alterations were useful, good, or sensible, they are unacceptable in principle, and the very idea of arbitrating between a creator's version and one by his corrector (censor, adapter) is perverse. Without a doubt, this or that sentence of *À la recherche du temps perdu* could be better written. But where could you find the lunatic who would want to read an improved Proust?

Besides, Kovarovic's alterations are anything but good or sensible. As proof of their soundness, Vogel cites the last scene of the opera, where, after the discovery of her murdered child and the arrest of her stepmother, Jenufa is alone with Laca. Jealous of her love for Steva, his half-brother Laca had earlier slashed Jenufa's face; now Jenufa forgives him: it was

out of love that he had injured her, just as she herself
had sinned out of love:

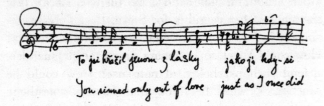

The allusion to her love for Steva, "as I once did,"
is delivered very rapidly, like a short cry, in high notes
that rise and break off; as if Jenufa is evoking something she wants to forget immediately. Kovarovic
broadens the melody of this passage (he "makes it
bloom," as Vogel says) by transforming it like this:

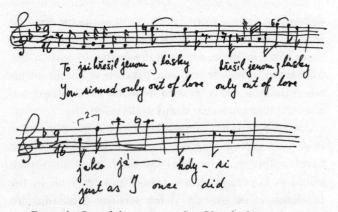

Doesn't Jenufa's song, asks Vogel, become more
beautiful under Kovarovic's pen? And isn't it still completely Janacekian? Yes, if you wanted to fake Janacek,
you couldn't do better. Nonetheless, the added melody
is absurd. Whereas in Janacek, Jenufa recalls her "sin"
rapidly, with suppressed horror, in Kovarovic she

grows tender at the recollection, she lingers over it, she is moved by it (her song stretches out the words "love," "I," and "once did"). So there to Laca's face she sings of her yearning for Steva, Laca's rival—she sings of her love for Steva, the cause of all her misery! How could Vogel, a passionate supporter of Janacek's, defend such psychological nonsense? How could he sanction it, when he knew that Janacek's aesthetic rebellion is rooted precisely in his rejection of the psychological unrealism current in opera practice? How is it possible to love someone and at the same time misunderstand him so completely?

4

Still—and here Vogel is right—by making the opera a little more conventional, Kovarovic's alterations did contribute to its success. "Let us distort you a bit, Maestro, and they'll love you." But there comes a time when the maestro refuses to be loved at such cost and would rather be detested and understood.

What means does an author have at his disposal to make himself understood for what he is? Hermann Broch hadn't many in the 1930s and in an Austria cut off from Germany turned fascist, nor later on in the loneliness of emigration: a few lectures explaining his aesthetic of the novel; then letters to friends, to his readers, to his publishers, to his translators; he left nothing undone, taking great care, for instance, over the copy on his book jackets. In a letter to his publisher, he protests a proposal for a promotional line on the back cover of his novel *The Sleepwalkers* that would compare him to

Hugo von Hofmannsthal and Italo Svevo. His counter-proposal: that he be compared to Joyce and Gide.

Let's look at this proposal: what is actually the difference between the Broch-Svevo-Hofmannsthal context and the Broch-Joyce-Gide context? The first context is *literary* in the broad, diffuse sense of the word; the second is specifically *novelistic* (the Gide of *The Counterfeiters* is the one Broch is claiming connection to). The first context is a *small context*—that is, local, Central European. The second is a *large context*—that is, international, global. By setting himself alongside Joyce and Gide, Broch is demanding that his novel be seen in the context of the *European novel*; he is aware that *The Sleepwalkers*, like *Ulysses* or *The Counterfeiters*, is a work that revolutionizes the novel form, that creates a new aesthetic of the novel, and that can be understood only against the backdrop of the history of the *novel as such*.

This demand of Broch's is valid for every important work. I can't repeat it too often: the value and the meaning of a work can be appreciated only in the greater international context. That truth becomes particularly pressing for any artist who is relatively isolated. A French surrealist, a *"nouveau roman"* author, a naturalistic nineteenth-century writer—all were borne along by a generation, by a movement, known throughout the world; their aesthetic program preceded their work, so to speak. But what about Gombrowicz—where do we put him? How are people to understand his aesthetic?

He left his country in 1939, at the age of thirty-five. For his credential as an artist, he brought with him only one book, his novel *Ferdydurke*, an ingenious

work barely known in Poland, totally unknown elsewhere. He landed far from Europe, in Argentina. He
was unimaginably alone. The great Argentine writers
never came near him. Later, the Polish anti-Communist
émigrés had little curiosity about his art. For fourteen
years, nothing happened to him, and then in 1953 he
began to write and publish his *Diary*. It doesn't tell us
much about his life, it is primarily a statement of his
position, a continuing aesthetic and philosophic self-
interpretation, a handbook on his "strategy"—or better
yet, it is his testament; not that he was thinking, at the
time, of his death: but as a last, definitive wish he
wanted to establish his own understanding of himself
and his work.

He demarcated his position by three key refusals: a
refusal to submit to engagement in Polish émigré politics (not that he had pro-Communist sympathies but
because the principle of politically engaged art was
repugnant to him); a refusal of Polish tradition (one
can make something worthwhile for Poland, he said,
only by opposing "Polishness," by shaking off its
heavy Romantic legacy); lastly, a refusal of the
Western modernism of the 1950s and '60s—a modernism he saw as sterile, "unfaithful to reality," inef-
fectual in the art of the novel, academic, snobbish,
absorbed in its self-theorizing (not that Gombrowicz
was less modern, but his modernism was different in
nature). That third "clause of the testament" is most
important and decisive—and is also doggedly misun-
derstood.

Ferdydurke was published in 1937, a year before
Nausea, but as Gombrowicz was unknown and Sartre
famous, *Nausea*, so to speak, usurped Gombrowicz's

rightful place in the history of the novel. Whereas
Nausea is existential philosophy in a novel's clothing
(as if a professor had decided to entertain his drowsy
students by teaching the lesson in the form of a novel),
Gombrowicz wrote a real novel that ties into the old
comic-novel tradition (as in Rabelais, Cervantes,
Fielding), and so existential issues, about which he was
no less passionate than Sartre, come across in his book
as unserious and funny.

Ferdydurke is one of those major works (along with
The Sleepwalkers and *The Man Without Qualities*)
that I see as inaugurating the "third (or overtime)
period" of the novel's history, by reviving the forgotten
experience of the pre-Balzac novel and by taking over
domains previously reserved for philosophy. That
Nausea, not *Ferdydurke*, became the exemplar of that
new orientation has had unfortunate consequences: the
wedding night of philosophy and the novel was spent
in mutual boredom. Discovered some twenty or thirty
years after their creation, Gombrowicz's works, and
Broch's and Musil's (and certainly Kafka's), no longer
had the potency required to seduce a generation and
create a movement; interpreted by a different aesthetic
school, which in many regards stood opposed to them,
they were respected—even admired—but ill understood, such that the greatest shift in the history of the
twentieth-century novel went unnoticed.

5

As I've said before, this was also the case with Janacek.
Max Brod put himself at Janacek's service as he had at

Kafka's: with selfless ardor. He deserves praise: he gave himself over to the two greatest artists ever to live in my native land. Kafka and Janacek: both underrated; both with an aesthetic difficult to apprehend; both victims of the pettiness of their milieu. Prague represented an enormous handicap for Kafka. He was isolated there from the German literary and publishing world, and that was fatal for him. His publishers concerned themselves very little with this author whom they barely knew personally. In a book on this problem, Joachim Unseld, the son of a leading German publisher, shows that the most likely reason (I consider the idea very realistic) why Kafka left his novels unfinished is that no one was asking him for them. Because if an author has no definite prospect of publishing his manuscript, nothing forces him to put the finishing touches on it, nothing keeps him from moving it off his desk for the time being and going on to something else.

To the Germans, Prague was just a provincial town, like Brno to the Czechs. Both Kafka and Janacek were therefore provincials. Kafka was nearly unknown in this country whose population was alien to him, while Janacek, in the same country, was trivialized by his own people.

Anyone who wants to understand the aesthetic incompetence of the founder of Kafkology should read Brod's monograph on Janacek. An enthusiastic work, it was certainly a great help to the underrated master. But how weak it is, how naïve! with its lofty words—"cosmos," "love," "compassion," "humiliated and insulted," "divine music," "hypersensitive soul," "tender soul," "soul of a dreamer"—and without the slightest structural analysis, the slightest attempt to get at the particular aesthetic of Janacek's music. Knowing musical Prague's hatred for the composer from the provinces, Brod wanted to prove that Janacek belonged to the national tradition and that he was every bit as good as the great Smetana, idol of the Czech national ideology. He became so obsessed by this provincial, narrow-minded, Czech-focused polemic that the rest of world music slipped out of his book, and of all composers of all periods, the only one mentioned is Smetana.

Ah, Max, Max! It's no good rushing into the other team's territory! All you'll find there are a hostile mob and bribed referees! Brod failed to utilize his position as a non-Czech to place Janacek in the *large context*, the cosmopolitan context of European music, the only one where he could be defended and understood; he locked him back within his national horizon, cut him off from modern music, and sealed his isolation. Such first interpretations stick to a work, it never shakes them off. Just as Brod's ideas would forever color all the literature on Kafka, so Janacek would forever suffer from the provincialization inflicted on him by his compatriots and confirmed by Brod.

Brod the enigma. He loved Janacek; he was guided by no ulterior motive, only by the spirit of justice; he loved him for the essential, for his art. But he did not understand that art.

I will never get to the bottom of the Brod mystery. And Kafka?—what did he think? In his 1911 diary, he tells this story: one day the two of them went to see a cubist painter, Willi Nowak, who had just finished a series of lithograph portraits of Brod; in the Picasso pattern as we know it, the first drawing was realistic, whereas the others, says Kafka, moved further and further off from their subject and wound up extremely abstract. Brod was uncomfortable; he didn't like any of the drawings except for the realistic first one, which, by contrast, pleased him greatly because, Kafka notes with tender irony, "beyond its looking like him, it had noble and serene lines around the mouth and eyes. . . ."

Brod understood cubism as little as he understood Kafka and Janacek. Doing his best to free them from their social isolation, he confirmed their *aesthetic aloneness*. The real meaning of his devotion to them was: even a person who loved them, and thus was most disposed to understand them, was alien to their art.

6

I am always surprised by people's amazement over Kafka's (alleged) decision to destroy all his work. As if such a decision were a priori absurd. As if an author could not have reasons enough to take his work along with him on his last voyage.

It could in fact happen that on final assessment the author realizes that he dislikes his books. And that he does not want to leave behind him this dismal monument of his failure. I know, I know, you'll object he is mistaken, that he is giving in to an unhealthy depression, but your exhortations are meaningless. He's in his own house with that work, not you, my dear fellow!

Another plausible reason: the author still loves his work but not the world. He can't bear the idea of leaving the work here to the mercy of a future he considers hateful.

And yet another possibility: the author still loves his work and doesn't even think about the future of the world, but having had his own experiences with the public, he understands the *vanitas vanitatum* of art, the inevitable incomprehension that is his lot, the incomprehension (not underestimation, I'm not talking about personal vanity) he has suffered during his lifetime and that he doesn't want to go on suffering post mortem. (It may incidentally be only the brevity of life that keeps artists from understanding fully the futility of their labor and making arrangements in time for the obliteration of both their work and themselves.)

Aren't these all valid reasons? Of course. Yet they weren't Kafka's reasons: he was aware of the value of what he was writing, he had no declared repugnance for the world, and—too young and nearly unknown—he had had no bad experiences with the public, having had almost none at all.

7

Kafka's testament: not a testament in the precise legal sense; actually two private letters; and not even true letters, in that they were never posted. Brod, who was Kafka's legal executor, found them after his friend's death, in 1924, in a drawer among a mass of other papers: one in ink, folded and addressed to Brod, the other more detailed and written in pencil. In his "Postscript to the First Edition" of *The Trial*, Brod explains: "In 1921 . . . I told my friend that I had made a will in which I asked him to destroy certain things [*dieses und jenes vernichten*], to look through

some others, and so forth. Kafka thereupon showed me
the outside of the note written in ink which was later
found in his desk, and said: 'My last testament will be
very simple: a request that you burn everything.' I can
still remember the exact wording of the answer I gave
him: '. . . I'm telling you right now that I won't carry
out your wishes.'" Brod evokes this recollection to justify disobeying his friend's testamentary wish; Kafka,
he continues, "knew what fanatical veneration I had
for his every word"; so he was well aware that he
would not be obeyed and he "should have chosen
another executor if his own instructions were uncondi-
tionally and finally in earnest." But is that so certain?
In his own testament, Brod was asking Kafka "to
destroy certain things"; why then wouldn't Kafka have
considered it normal to request the same service of
Brod? And if Kafka really knew that he would not be
obeyed, why, after their conversation in 1921, did he
write that second, penciled letter, in which he elaborates his instructions and makes them specific? But
let's drop it: we'll never know what these two young
friends said to each other on a subject that was, by the
way, not their most urgent concern, since neither one
of them, and Kafka especially, could at the time consider himself in serious danger of immortality.

It's often said: if Kafka really wished to destroy
what he had written, he would have destroyed it himself. But how? His letters were in the hands of the
recipients. (He himself kept none of the letters he
received.) It's true that he could have burned his
diaries. But they were working diaries (more notebooks than diaries), they were useful to him for as long
as he was writing, and he wrote until his very last

days. The same can be said of his unfinished works. Only in the event of death would they be irremediably unfinished; while he was still alive he could always get back to them. Not even a story he considers a failure is useless to a writer, as it can become material for another story. As long as he is not dying, a writer has no reason to destroy something he has written. But when Kafka was dying he was no longer in his home, he was in a sanatorium and unable to destroy anything, he could only count on a friend's help. And not having many friends, having finally but one, he counted on him.

People also say that wanting to destroy one's own work is a pathological act. In that case, disobeying Kafka's destructive wish becomes loyalty to the other Kafka, the creator. This touches on the greatest lie of the legend surrounding his testament: Kafka did not want to destroy his work. He expressed himself with utter precision in the second of those letters: "Of all my writings, only the books are worthwhile [*gelten*]: *Judgment*, *Stoker*, *Metamorphosis*, *Penal Colony*, *Country Doctor*, and a story: 'Hunger Artist.' (The few copies of *Meditations* can stay, I don't want to put anyone to the trouble of pulping them, but nothing from that book is to be reprinted.)" Thus, not only did Kafka not repudiate his work, but he actually assessed it and tried to separate what should survive (what could be reprinted) from what fell short of his standards; there is sadness, severity, but no insanity, no blindness of despair, in his judgment: he finds all his published books worthwhile except the first, *Meditations*, probably considering it immature (that would be hard to contradict). His rejection does not automatically concern everything unpublished, for he includes among the "worthwhile" works the story "A Hunger Artist," which at the time he wrote the letter existed only in manuscript. Later on, he added to that piece three more stories ("First Sorrow," "A Little Woman," and "Josefine the Singer") to make a book; he was correcting the proofs of this book in the sanatorium on his deathbed—nearly poignant evidence that Kafka had nothing to do with the legend of the author wanting to destroy his work.

His wish to destroy thus concerns only two clearly defined categories of writing:

—in the first place, most emphatically: the personal writings: letters, diaries;

—in the second place: the stories and the novels he had not, in his judgment, succeeded in bringing off.

8

I am looking at a window across the way. Toward evening the light goes on. A man enters the room. Head lowered, he paces back and forth; from time to time he runs his hand through his hair. Then, suddenly, he realizes that the lights are on and he can be seen. Abruptly, he pulls the curtain. Yet he wasn't counterfeiting money in there; he had nothing to hide but himself, the way he walked around the room, the sloppy way he was dressed, the way he stroked his hair. His well-being depended on his freedom from being seen.

Shame is one of the key notions of the Modern Era, the individualistic period that is imperceptibly receding from us these days; shame: an epidermal instinct to defend one's personal life; to require a curtain over the window; to insist that a letter addressed to A not be read by B. One of the elementary situations in the passage to adulthood, one of the prime conflicts with parents, is the claim to a drawer for letters and notebooks, the claim to a drawer with a key; we enter adulthood through *the rebellion of shame*.

An old revolutionary utopia, whether fascist or communist: life without secrets, where public life and private life are one and the same. The surrealist dream André Breton loved: the glass house, a house without curtains where man lives in full view of the world. Ah, the beauty of transparency! The only successful realization of this dream: a society totally monitored by the police.

I wrote about this in *The Unbearable Lightness of Being*: Jan Prochazka, an important figure of the Prague Spring, came under heavy surveillance after the Russian invasion of 1968. At the time, he saw a good deal of another great opposition figure, Professor Vaclav Cerny, with whom he liked to drink and talk. All their conversations were secretly recorded, and I suspect the two friends knew it and didn't give a damn. But one day in 1970 or 1971, with the intent to discredit Prochazka, the police began to broadcast these conversations as a radio serial. For the police it was an audacious, unprecedented act. And, surprisingly: it nearly succeeded; instantly Prochazka *was* discredited: because in private, a person says all sorts of things, slurs friends, uses coarse language, acts silly, tells dirty jokes, repeats himself, makes a companion laugh by shocking him with outrageous talk, floats heretical ideas he'd never admit in public, and so forth. Of course, we all act like Prochazka, in private we bad-mouth our friends and use coarse language; that we act different in private than in public is everyone's most conspicuous experience, it is the very ground of the life of the individual; curiously, this obvious fact remains unconscious, unacknowledged, forever obscured by lyrical dreams of the transparent glass house, it is rarely understood to be the value one must defend beyond all others. Thus only gradually did people realize (though their rage was all the greater) that the real scandal was not Prochazka's daring talk but the rape of his life; they realized (as if by electric shock) that private and public are two essentially different worlds and that respect for that difference is the indispensable condition, the sine qua non, for a man to live free; that the curtain separating these two worlds is not to be tampered with, and that curtain-rippers are criminals. And because the curtain-rippers were serving a hated regime, they were unanimously held to be particularly contemptible criminals.

When I arrived in France from that Czechoslovakia bristling with microphones, I saw on a magazine cover a large photo of Jacques Brel hiding his face from the photographers who had tracked him down in front of the hospital where he was being treated for his already advanced cancer. And suddenly I felt I was encountering the very same evil that had made me flee my country; broadcasting Prochazka's conversations and photographing a dying singer hiding his face seemed to belong to the same world; I said to myself that *when it becomes the custom and the rule* to divulge another person's private life, we are entering a time when the highest stake is the survival or the disappearance of the individual.

9

There are almost no trees in Iceland, and the few that exist are all in the cemeteries; as if there were no dead without trees, as if there were no trees without the dead. They are not planted alongside the grave, as in idyllic Central Europe, but right in the center of it, to force a passerby to imagine the roots down below piercing the body. I am walking with Elvar D. in the Reykjavik cemetery; he stops at a grave whose tree is still quite small; barely a year ago his friend was buried; he starts reminiscing aloud about him: his private life was marked by some secret, probably a sexual one. "Because secrets excite such irritated curiosity, my wife, my daughters, the people around me, all insisted I tell them about it. To such an extent that my relations with my wife have been bad ever since. I couldn't forgive her aggressive curiosity, and she couldn't forgive my silence, which to her was evidence of how little I trusted her." He smiled, and then: "I divulged nothing," he said. "Because I had nothing to divulge. I had forbidden myself to want to know my friend's secrets, and I didn't know them." I listened to him with fascination: since childhood I had heard it said that a friend is the person with whom you share your secrets and who even has the right, in the name of friendship, to insist on knowing them. For my Icelander, friendship is something else: it is standing guard at the door behind which your friend keeps his private life hidden; it is being the person who never opens that door; who allows no one else to open it.

10

I think of the ending of *The Trial*: the two men bend over K. and one of them thrusts a knife deep into his heart: "With failing eyes K. could still see, right near his face, the two men cheek by jowl watching the outcome: 'Like a dog!' he said; it was as if the shame of it must outlive him."

The last noun in *The Trial*: "shame." Its last image: the faces of two strangers, close by his own face, almost touching it, watching K.'s most intimate state, his death throes. In that last noun, in that last image, is concentrated the entire novel's fundamental situation: being accessible at any time in his bedroom; having his breakfast eaten by other people; being available, day and night, to go where he's summoned; seeing his window curtains confiscated; being unable to see whom he wants; no longer being his own man; losing his status as an individual. This *transformation of a man from subject to object* is experienced as shame.

I don't believe that Kafka asked Brod to destroy his letters because he feared their publication. Such an idea could scarcely have entered his mind. The publishers were not interested in his novels, why would they have cared about his letters? What made him want to destroy them was shame, simple shame, not that of a writer but that of an ordinary individual, the shame of leaving private things lying about for the eyes of others—of the family, of strangers—the shame of being turned into an object, the shame that could "outlive him."

And yet Brod made these letters public; earlier, in his own will and testament, he had asked Kafka "to destroy certain things"; and here he himself published *everything*, indiscriminately; even that long, painful letter found in a drawer, the letter that Kafka never decided to send to his father and that, thanks to Brod, anyone but its addressee could eventually read. To me, Brod's indiscretion is inexcusable. He betrayed his friend. He acted against his friend's wishes, against the meaning and the spirit of his wishes, against the sense of shame he knew in the man.

11

There is an essential difference between the novel on the one hand and memoirs, biography, autobiography, on the other. A biography's value lies in the newness and accuracy of the real facts it reveals. A novel's value is in the revelation of previously unseen possibilities of existence as such; in other words, the novel uncovers what is hidden in each of us. A common form of praise for a novel is to say: I see myself in that character; I have the sense that the author knows me and is writing about me; or as a grievance: I feel attacked, laid bare, humiliated by this novel. We should never mock such apparently naïve judgments: they prove that the novel is being read as a novel.

That is why the roman à clef (which deals with real people with the intention of making them recognizable beneath fictional names) is a false novel, an aesthetically equivocal thing, morally unclean. Kafka disguised under the name Garta! You object to the author: "That's not accurate!" The author: "These aren't memoirs I've written; Garta is an imaginary character!" You: "As an imaginary character, he's implausible, badly made, written with no talent!" The author: "But this isn't the usual sort of character; he lets me make new revelations about my friend Kafka!" You: "Inaccurate revelations!" The author: "These aren't memoirs I've written; Garta is an imaginary character!. . . " And so on.

Of course, every novelist, intentionally or not, draws on his own life; there are entirely invented characters, created out of pure reverie; there are those inspired by a model, sometimes directly, more often indirectly; there are those created from a single detail observed in some person; and all of them owe much to the author's introspection, to his self-knowledge. The work of the imagination transforms these inspirations and observations so thoroughly that the novelist forgets about them. Yet before publishing his book, he must think to hide the keys that might make them detectable; first, out of the minimum of consideration due persons who, to their surprise, will find fragments of their lives in the novel, and second, because keys (true or false) one puts into the reader's hands can only mislead him: instead of unknown aspects of existence, he will be searching a novel for unknown aspects of the author's existence; the entire meaning of the art of the novel will thus be annihilated, as it was annihilated, for instance, by that American professor who, wielding his huge bunch of skeleton keys, wrote the big biography of Hemingway:

Through the force of his interpretation, he turned Hemingway's whole oeuvre into a single roman à clef; as if it had been turned inside out like a jacket: suddenly, the books are invisible inside, and on the lining outside, a reader avidly observes the (real or alleged) events of the life—trivial, painful, ridiculous, pedestrian, stupid, petty events; thus the work is undone, the imaginary characters are transformed into people from the author's life, and the biographer begins the moral trial of the writer: in one short story there is a wicked mother character: Hemingway is maligning his own mother here; in another story there is a cruel father: it is Hemingway's revenge on his father for allowing his childhood tonsils to be removed without anesthesia; in "Cat in the Rain," the unnamed female character "is dissatisfied with her. . . self-absorbed, unresponsive husband": this is Hemingway's wife Hadley, complaining; the female character of "Summer People" is to be seen as the wife of Dos Passos: Hemingway tried in vain to seduce her and, in the story, he abuses her disgracefully by making love to her in the guise of a character; in *Across the River and Into the Trees*, an unnamed, very ugly man appears in a bar: Hemingway is describing the ugliness of Sinclair Lewis, who, "bitterly hurt and angered by Hemingway's cruelest passage, died three months after the novel was published." And so on and on, one denunciation after another.

Novelists have always resisted that *biographical furor* whose representative prototype, according to Proust, is Sainte-Beuve with his motto: "I do not look on literature as a thing apart, or, at least, detachable, from the rest of the man. . . ." Understanding a work therefore requires knowing the man first—that is, Sainte-Beuve specifies, knowing the answers to a certain number of questions even though they "might seem at the furthest remove from the nature of his writings: What were his religious views? How did he react to the sight of nature? How did he conduct himself in regard to women, in regard to money? Was he rich, was he poor? What governed his actions, what was his daily way of life? What was his vice, or his weakness?" This quasi-police method, Proust comments, requires a critic "to surround himself with every possible piece of information about a writer, to check his letters, to interrogate people who knew him. . . ."

Yet, surrounded as he was "with every possible piece of information," Sainte-Beuve managed not to recognize any of the great writers of his time—not Balzac nor Stendhal nor Flaubert nor Baudelaire; by studying their lives he inevitably missed their work, because, said Proust, "a book is the product of a *self other* than the self we manifest in our habits, in our social life, in our vices"; "the writer's true self is manifested in his books *alone*."

Proust's polemic against Sainte-Beuve is of fundamental importance. Let us make clear: Proust is not criticizing Sainte-Beuve for exaggerating; he is not decrying the limitations of Sainte-Beuve's method; his verdict is absolute: that method is blind to the author's *other self*; blind to his aesthetic wishes; incompatible with art; directed against art; hostile to art.

12

In France, Kafka's work is published in four volumes. The second volume: stories and narrative fragments; that is: everything Kafka published in his lifetime, plus everything found in his desk drawers: unpublished and incomplete stories, drafts, false starts, rejected or abandoned versions. What order should it all have? The editor applied two principles: (1) with no distinction as to their nature, genre, or degree of completion, all the narrative writings are set on an equal plane and (2) arranged in chronological order, that is, in the order of their birth.

This is why none of the three collections of stories Kafka himself put together for publication (*Meditations, A Country Doctor, A Hunger Artist*) is presented here in France in the form Kafka gave them; these collections have simply disappeared; the individual stories constituting them are scattered among other things (among drafts, fragments, and such) by chronology; thus eight hundred pages of Kafka's writings become a flood where everything dissolves into everything else, a flood formless as only water can be, water that flows and carries along with it both good and bad, finished and unfinished, strong and weak, draft and work.

Brod had already proclaimed the "fanatical veneration" with which he surrounded each of Kafka's words.

The editors of Kafka's work show the same *absolute veneration* for everything their author touched. But understand the mystery of absolute veneration: it is also, and inevitably, the absolute denial of the author's aesthetic wishes. For aesthetic wishes show not only by what an author has written but also by what he has deleted. Deleting a paragraph calls for even more talent, cultivation, and creative power than writing it does. Therefore, publishing what the author deleted is the same act of rape as censoring what he decided to retain.

What obtains for deletions within the microcosm of a particular work also obtains for deletions within the macrocosm of a complete body of work. There too, as he assesses his work, and guided by his aesthetic requirements, the author often excludes what doesn't satisfy him. Claude Simon, for instance, no longer allows his earliest books to be reprinted. Faulkner explicitly stated his wish to leave no trace "but the printed books," in other words, none of what the *garbage-can scavengers* would find after his death. He thus made the same request as Kafka, and he was obeyed the same way: they published everything they could dig up. I purchase Seiji Ozawa's recording of Mahler's First Symphony. This four-movement symphony originally had five movements, but after the premiere Mahler definitively removed the second, which is not to be found in any printed score. Ozawa put it back into the symphony; so now absolutely everyone can see that Mahler was right to delete it. Need I go on? The list is endless.

The way Kafka's collected works were published in

France shocks no one; it corresponds to the spirit of the time: "Kafka is to be read as a whole," the editor explains; "among his various modes of expression, none can claim greater worth than the others. Such is the decision of the posterity we are; it is an acknowledged judgment and one that must be accepted. Sometimes we go further: not only do we reject any hierarchy among genres but we deny the very existence of genres, we assert that Kafka speaks the same language throughout his work. In Kafka is finally achieved the situation everywhere sought or always hoped for—a perfect correspondence between lived experience and literary expression."

"Perfect correspondence between lived experience and literary expression." This is a variant of Sainte-Beuve's slogan: "Literature inseparable from its author." A slogan that recalls: "The unity of life and work." Which evokes the famous line wrongly attributed to Goethe: "Life like a work of art." These magical catchphrases are simultaneously statements of the obvious (of course what a man does is inseparable from him), countertruths (inseparable or not, the creation surpasses the life), and lyrical clichés (the unity of life and work "everywhere sought or always hoped for" is presented as an ideal state, a utopia, a lost paradise at last regained), but most important, they reveal the wish to refuse art its autonomous status, to force it back into its source, into the author's life, to dilute it there and thus deny its raison d'être (if a life can be a work of art, what use are works of art?). The sequence Kafka chose for the stories in his collections is disregarded because the only sequence considered valid is that dictated by life itself. No one cares about the artist

Kafka, who troubles us with his puzzling aesthetic, because we'd rather have Kafka as the fusion of experience and work, the Kafka who had a difficult relationship with his father and didn't know how to deal with women. Hermann Broch protested when his work was put into a *small context* with Svevo and Hofmannsthal. Poor Kafka, he wasn't granted even that small context. When people speak of him, they don't mention Hofmannsthal, or Mann, or Musil, or Broch; they leave him only one context: Felice, the father, Milena, Dora; he is flung back into the *mini-mini-mini-context* of his biography, far from the history of the novel, very far from art.

13

The Modern Era made man—the individual, a thinking ego—into the basis of everything. From that new conception of the world came a new conception of the work of art as well. It became the original expression of a unique individual. It is in art that the individualism of the Modern Era was realized and confirmed, found its expression, its consecration, its glory, its monument.

If a work of art emanates from an individual and his uniqueness, it is logical that this unique being, the author, should possess all rights over the thing that emanates exclusively from him. After a centuries-long process, these rights attained their definitive form during the French Revolution, which recognized literary property as "the most sacred, the most personal of all property."

I remember the days when I was enchanted by Moravian folk music: the beauty of its melodic phrases; the originality of its metaphors. How are such songs born? Collectively? No; that art had its anonymous individual creators, its village poets and composers, but once their invention was released into the world, they had no way of following after it and protecting it against changes, distortions, endless metamorphoses. At the time, I was much like those who looked upon such a world with no artistic-property claims as a kind of paradise; a paradise where poetry was made by all and for all.

I evoke this memory to point out that the great figure of the Modern Era, the author, emerged only gradually over these recent centuries and that in the history of humanity, the era of authors' rights is a fleeting moment, brief as a photoflash. And yet, without the prestige of the author and his rights, the great blossoming of European art in recent centuries would be inconceivable, and so would Europe's greatest glory. Its greatest or perhaps its only glory, because, if reminder is needed, it's not for its generals or its statesmen that Europe was admired even by those it caused to suffer.

For authors' rights to become law, it required a certain frame of mind that was inclined to respect the author. That frame of mind, which took shape slowly over the centuries, seems to be coming undone lately. If not, they couldn't accompany a toilet paper commercial with a passage from a Brahms symphony. Or be praised for publishing abridged versions of Stendhal novels. If there were still a frame of mind that respects the author, people would wonder: Would Brahms agree to this? Wouldn't Stendhal be angry?

I examine the new version of the French law on authors' rights: the problems of writers, composers, painters, poets, novelists take up a minute part of it, most of the text being devoted to the great industry called "audiovisual." There's no question this immense industry requires entirely new rules of the game. Because the situation has changed: what we persist in calling "art" is less and less the "original expression of a unique individual." How can the screenwriter for a film that costs millions prevail with his own moral rights (say, the right to prevent tampering with what he wrote) when involved in its creation is a battalion of other persons, who also consider themselves authors and whose moral rights are reciprocally limited by his; and how claim anything at all against the will of the producer, who though not an author is certainly the film's only real boss?

Even without their rights being restricted, authors in the old-style arts are suddenly thrust into another world where authors' rights are starting to lose their old aura. When a conflict arises in this new climate, those who violate authors' moral rights (adapters of novels; garbage-can scavengers who plunder great writers with their so-called critical editions; advertising that dissolves a thousand-year-old legacy in its bloody saliva; periodicals that reprint whatever they want without permission; producers who interfere with film-makers' work; stage directors who treat texts so freely that only a madman could still write for the theater; and so on) have general opinion on their side, whereas an author claiming his moral rights risks winding up without public sympathy and with judicial support that is rather grudging, for even the guardians of the laws are sensitive to the mood of the time.

I think of Stravinsky. Of his tremendous effort to preserve all his work in his own performances as an unimpeachable standard. Samuel Beckett behaved similarly: he took to attaching more and more detailed stage directions to his plays, and insisted (contrary to the usual tolerance) that they be strictly observed; he often attended rehearsals in order to evaluate the direction, and sometimes did it himself; he even published as a book the notes for his own production of *Endgame* in Germany so as to establish it for good. His publisher and friend, Jérôme Lindon, stands watch—if need be, to the point of lawsuit—to insure that his authorial wishes are respected even after his death.

Such major effort to give a work a definitive form, thoroughly worked out and supervised by the author, is unparalleled in history. It is as if Stravinsky and Beckett wanted to protect their work not only against the current practice of distortion but also against a future less and less likely to respect a text or a score; it is as if they hoped to provide an example, the ultimate example of the supreme concept of author: one who demands the *complete* realization of his aesthetic wishes.

14

Kafka sent the manuscript of "The Metamorphosis" to a magazine whose editor, Robert Musil, was prepared to publish it on the condition that the author shorten it. (Ah, sorry encounters between great writers!) Kafka's reaction was as glacial and as categoric as Stravinsky's to Ansermet. He could bear the idea of not being published at all, but the idea of being published and mutilated he found unbearable. His concept of authorship was as absolute as Stravinsky's or Beckett's, but whereas they more or less succeeded in imposing theirs, he failed to do so. This failure is a turning point in the history of authors' rights.

In 1925, when Brod published the two letters known as Kafka's testament in his "Postscript to the First Edition" of *The Trial*, he explained that Kafka knew full well that his wishes would not be fulfilled. Let us assume that Brod was telling the truth, that those two letters were indeed only expressing a bad mood, and that on the subject of any eventual (very improbable) posthumous publication of Kafka's writings, everything had been fully understood between the two friends; in that case, Brod, the executor, could take full responsibility upon himself and publish whatever he thought best; in that case, he had no moral obligation to inform us of Kafka's wishes, which, according to Brod, were not valid or were so no longer.

Yet he hastened to publish these "testamentary" letters and to give them as much impact as possible; actually, he had already begun to create the greatest work of his life, his myth of Kafka, one of whose crucial components is precisely that wish, unique in all of history—the wish of an author who would annihilate all his work. And thus is Kafka engraved on the public's memory. In accordance with what Brod gives us to believe in his mythographic novel, where, with no nuance whatever, Garta/Kafka would destroy *every-thing* he has written; because he is dissatisfied with it artistically? ah no, Brod's Kafka is a religious thinker; remember: wanting not to proclaim but "to live his faith," Garta granted no great importance to his writings, "mere rungs to help him climb to the heights." His friend, Nowy/Brod, refuses to obey him because even though what Garta wrote was "mere sketches," they could help "wandering humanity" in its quest for the path of righteousness to "something irreplaceable."

With Kafka's "testament," the great legend of Saint Kafka/Garta is born, and along with it a littler legend—of Brod his prophet, who with touching earnestness makes public his friend's last wish even as he confesses why, in the name of very lofty principles, he decided not to obey him. The great mythographer won his bet. His act was elevated to the rank of a great gesture worthy of emulation. For who could doubt Brod's loyalty to his friend? And who would dare doubt the value of every sentence, every word, every single syllable Kafka left to humanity?

And thus did Brod create the model for disobedience to dead friends; a judicial precedent for those who would circumvent an author's last wish or divulge his most intimate secrets.

15

With regard to the unfinished prose, I readily concede that it would put any executor in a very uncomfortable situation. For among these writings of varying significance are the three novels; and Kafka wrote nothing greater than these. Yet it is not at all abnormal that because they were unfinished he ranked them among his failures; an author has trouble believing that the value of a work he has not seen through to the end might already be almost fully discernible, before it is done. But what an author is incapable of seeing may be clear to the eyes of an outsider.

What would I myself have done in Brod's situation? For me a dead friend's wish is law; on the other hand, how could I destroy three novels I infinitely admire, novels without which I find the art of our own century unimaginable? No, I would have been incapable of obeying Kafka's instructions dogmatically and to the letter. I would not have destroyed these novels. I would have done everything to see them published. I would have acted with the certainty that, in the beyond, I would manage to persuade their author that I had betrayed neither him nor his work, whose perfecting was so important to him. But my disobedience (a disobedience strictly limited to these three novels) I would have considered an *exception* I had made on my own responsibility, at my own moral risk, and made as a person *violating a law*, not denying or nullifying it. That is why, aside from this exception, I would have faithfully, discreetly, and fully carried out all the wishes of Kafka's "testament."

16

A television broadcast: three famous and admired women collectively propose that women too should have the right to be buried in the Panthéon. It's important, they say, to consider the symbolic significance of this act. And they immediately suggest the names of some great dead women who, in their opinion, could be moved there.

A fair demand, certainly; yet something about it troubles me: these dead women who could be moved right over to the Panthéon, aren't they now lying beside their husbands? Certainly; and they wanted it so. What then are we to do with the husbands? Move them too? That would be hard; not being important enough, they must stay where they are, and the wives that have been moved out will spend their eternity in widows' solitude.

Then I say to myself: and what about the men already in the Panthéon? Yes, the men! Are they perchance in the Panthéon of their own will? It was after they died, without asking their opinion, and certainly contrary to their last wishes, that it was decided to turn them into symbols and separate them from their wives.

After Chopin's death, Polish patriots cut up his body to take out his heart. They nationalized this poor muscle and buried it in Poland.

A dead person is treated either as trash or as a symbol. Either way, it's the same disrespect to his vanished individuality.

17

Ah, it's so easy to disobey a dead person. If, nonetheless, we sometimes submit to his wishes, it is not out of fear, out of duress, but because we love him and refuse to believe him dead. If an old peasant on his deathbed begs his son not to cut down the old pear tree outside the window, the pear tree will not be cut down for as long as the son remembers his father with love.

This has little to do with any religious belief in the eternal life of the soul. It's simply that a dead person I love will never be dead for me. I can't even say: "I loved him"; no, it's: "I love him." And my refusing to speak of my love for him in the past tense means that the dead person *is*. That may be the seat of man's religious dimension. Indeed, obedience to a last wish is mysterious: it goes beyond all practical and rational thought: the old peasant will never know, in his grave, if the pear tree has been cut down or not; yet for the son who loves him, it is impossible to not obey him.

Long ago I was moved (I still am) by the end of Faulkner's novel *The Wild Palms*. The woman dies of a botched abortion, the man is in prison under a ten-year sentence; a white tablet, poison, is brought to him in his cell; but he quickly dismisses the idea of suicide, because his only way of prolonging the life of the beloved woman is to preserve her in his memory.

". . . so when she became not then half of memory became not and if I become not then all of remembering will cease to be.—Yes, he thought, between grief and nothing I will take grief."

Later on, writing *The Book of Laughter and Forgetting*, I immersed myself in the character Tamina, who has lost her husband and is trying desperately to recover, to gather, scattered memories so as to reconstruct a person who has disappeared, a bygone past; it was then that I began to understand that a memory doesn't give us back the dead person's *presence*; memories are only confirmation of his absence; in memories the dead person is only a past that is fading, receding, inaccessible.

Yet if it is impossible for me ever to regard as dead the being I love, how will his presence be manifested?

In his wishes, which I know and with which I will keep faith. I think of the old pear tree that will stand outside the window for as long as the peasant's son shall live.